T0352669

CATERPILLAR
BY ALISON CARR

Caterpillar had its world premiere at Theatre503 in London on
3 September 2018 ahead of its transfer to the Stephen Joseph Theatre
in Scarborough, produced by Small Truth Theatre in association with
Theatre503 and Michelle Barnette Productions.

Supported using public funding by
**ARTS COUNCIL
ENGLAND**

LOTTERY FUNDED

CATERPILLAR

BY ALISON CARR

CAST

Claire	Judith Amsenga
Maeve	Tricia Kelly
Simon	Alan Mahon

CREATIVE TEAM

Director	Yasmeen Arden
Producer	Michelle Barnette
Executive Producer	Jamie Arden
Set and Costume Designer	Holly Pigott
Lighting Designer	Ben Jacobs
Sound Designer	Jac Cooper
Stage Manager	Abi Toghill
PR	Flavia Fraser-Cannon for Mobius

BIOGRAPHIES

JUDITH AMSENGA | CLAIRE
Judith Amsenga trained at LAMDA.

Theatre includes: *Allen Key, Caravantomime* (The Caravan Theatre); *The Golden Dragon* (tour, ATC); *Mixed Up North* (tour, Out of Joint); *Mr Turner* (Tin Man Productions); *Scars* by Vivienne Franzmann (Theater Utrecht); *Home Death* (Finborough) and *On the Line* (Arcola), as well as being the voice of various audiobooks (Pinewood Studios). She is one of the co-founders of The Nursery Theatre.

TRICIA KELLY | MAEVE
Theatre includes: *Death of a Salesman* (Royal & Derngate/tour); *The Kitchen* (National Theatre); *Julius Caesar, Ion* (RSC); *The Life and Adventures of Nicholas Nickleby* (West End/Chichester & UK tour/Toronto); *The Lower Depths, Uncle Vanya, Pieces of Vincent* (Arcola); *Tiger Country, The Maths Tutor* (Hampstead); *Man to Man* (Park/Mercury Colchester); *Hope Place* (Liverpool Everyman); *Responsible Other* (Hampstead Downstairs); *Cannibals, The Gatekeeper* – Best Studio Performance nomination, Manchester Theatre Awards (Royal Exchange); *This Wide Night* (Bernie Grant); *Blue Heaven* (Finborough); *When We Are Married* (West Yorkshire/Liverpool Playhouse); *Unprotected* (Everyman/Traverse); *Some Explicit Polaroids* (Out of Joint – UK and US tour); *Inland Sea* (Wilton's Music Hall); *Local* (Royal Court Theatre Upstairs); *A Wife Without a Smile, The House Among the Stars, The Way of the World, The Choice* (Orange Tree); *Much Ado About Nothing, The Seagull, The Government Inspector, As You Like It* (Sheffield Crucible); *Barbarians, Dancing at Lughnasa, Jamaica Inn* (Salisbury); *Season's Greetings, A Whisper of Angel's Wings, Julius Caesar* (Birmingham Rep); *King Lear, Not I, Two, Sunsets and Glories* (West Yorkshire Playhouse); *The Voysey Inheritance* (Edinburgh Lyceum); *Amphytryon* (The Gate); *Venus and Lucrece* (Almeida); *Victory* (Wrestling School/Greenwich); *Seven Lears, Golgo, Et in Arcadia Ego, The Last Supper* (Wrestling School/Royal Court); *A Mouthful of Birds, Deadlines, Fen* (also New York) (Joint Stock/Royal Court); *Top Girls* (Lancaster); *The Country Wife, Just Between Ourselves* (Belgrade) and *Saturday Night and Sunday Morning* (Nottingham Playhouse).

TV and film includes: *The Committee, Carnage, Doctors, EastEnders, My Family, Casualty, The Bill, High Stakes, In Sickness and in Health, This is David Landor, The Josie Lawrence Show, It's History, Gran, Christobel, Dangerous Lady, A Small Dance, Top Dog, Real Lies.*

ALAN MAHON | SIMON
Alan Mahon trained at The Lir Academy, Dublin.

Theatre includes *Alkaline* (Park); *If We Got Some More Cocaine I Could Show You How I Love You* (Project Arts Centre/tour 2018; Old Red Lion 2016); *Brutal Cessation* (Edinburgh Fringe/Theatre503); *Hamlet, All's Well That Ends Well* (Tobacco Factory/tour); *King Lear* (Second Age); *The Windstealers* (Dublin Fringe); *The Waste Ground Party, Burial at Thebes* (Abbey, Dublin).

TV and film includes *Resistance* (RTÉ/Netflix); *No Dogs* (short) and *Fair City* (RTÉ).

Alan co-founded and runs One Duck, a Dublin-based theatre company.

ALISON CARR | WRITER

Alison Carr recently completed an attachment with the National Theatre and her credits include *Hush* (Paines Plough/RWCMD/The Gate); *Iris* (Live Theatre, winner Journal Culture Awards – Writer of the Year); *The Soaking of Vera Shrimp* (winner Live Theatre/Empty Space Bursary Award); *Fat Alice* (Traverse/Òran Mór/The Lemon Tree); *A Wondrous Place* (nominee Manchester Theatre Awards – Best Studio Production) and *Dolly Would* (BBC Radio 4). She is a member of the Traverse Fifty and a founder member of Forward Theatre Project with whom her work includes *Clothes Swap Theatre Party* (Derby Theatre) and *Can Cause Death* starring Olivier-Award winner David Bradley (National Theatre/ Latitude Festival/Northern Stage).

YASMEEN ARDEN | DIRECTOR

Yasmeen Arden is Artistic Director at Small Truth Theatre. Directing credits include the award-winning *The Three Sillies* (Arcola/Somersault/tour); *Poking the Bear* by Chris Bush, *Elexion* by Chloe Todd Fordham (Theatre503); *Over The Hill There's Something Better* by Sharon Clarke (New Diorama); *Dead Yard* by Matthew Turner (Playwrought/ LAB/Arcola); *We are Beautiful* by Brian Eley (Catalyst Festival), as well as site-specific work such as *On The Line* by Aled Pedrick (Ivy House/Merge Festival/Platform Southwark) and *The Unfortunates* on the streets of Watford for Watford Palace Theatre. Yasmeen recently directed Christopher Hogg for his TEDx Talk. Her production of *Nest* by Katy Warner, was described as 'one of the highlights' of VAULT Festival 2018.

MICHELLE BARNETTE | PRODUCER

Michelle Barnette is an independent theatre producer and general manager specialising in new writing. She holds two masters degrees from King's College London in Early Modern History and Shakespeare Studies in association with Shakespeare's Globe. Michelle has worked with the Westway Trust and the Kevin Spacey Foundation.

Work includes: *SPARKS* (VAULT Festival/Pleasance Edinburgh/HighTide Festivals); *Caterpillar* (Theatre503/Scarborough); *QU4RTER* (The Other Palace); *Love Me Now* (Tristan Bates); *Che: The Musical* (BEAM Festival); *The Sex Workers' Opera* (Ovalhouse/UK tour); *Brutal Cessation* (Assembly Edinburgh/Theatre503); *Dust* (Underbelly Edinburgh – winner of The Stage Award); *The Scar Test* (Soho Theatre/UK tour – shortlisted for the KSF Artist of Choice Award).

JAMIE ARDEN | EXECUTIVE PRODUCER

Jamie Arden is an experienced producer, theatre-maker and senior arts leader.

As well as Executive Producer for Small Truth Theatre, Jamie is Executive Director of Watford Palace Theatre (the premiere 600-seat regional producing house/ACE NPO in Hertfordshire) and is Director of two large-scale international outdoor festivals – Imagine Watford and Imagine Luton.

Prior roles include: General Manager at Arcola Theatre, Head of Operations & Head of Public Events at Shakespeare's Globe, National Programmes Manager at Anne Frank Trust/Anne Frank House, Managing Director at Realeyes. Jamie is also a fellow of the Imperial War Museum in London and originally trained at East15.

Key highlight credits include: as performer: *Billy Dobbs in Blagger* (Escape Artists/ROH, Volksbuhne, Ustinov Bath); as Theatre Director: *How to Be a Hero, Knightime* (Scratchbuilt/ Edinburgh Fringe); as Producer/Exec Producer: *Mare Rider* (Arcola/ Riksteatern/European tour); *The Three Sillies, Mirrorball* (Arcola/tour); *Little White Lies* (Waterloo East); *Dream Space* (Shakespeare's Globe/Royal & Derngate); *Jefferson's Garden, Coming Up, Poppy & George, Jane Wenham, Wipers, I Capture the Castle* (Watford Palace/tour).

HOLLY PIGOTT | SET AND COSTUME DESIGNER

Holly Pigott graduated from the Royal Welsh College of Music and Drama in 2011. She was a finalist in the Linbury Prize for Stage Design and also completed a year-long placement as a Trainee Designer with the Royal Shakespeare Company. Her design credits include: *La Scala Di Seta* (Linbury Studio, ROH); *The Island* (Young Vic/JMK Award); *Little Wolf* (Chapter Arts Centre); International Opera Awards 2017 and 2018 (London Coliseum); *The Moor* (Old Red Lion); *Skin A Cat* (Vault Festival/Bunker/UK tour); *Mad King Suibhne* (Bury Court Opera); *Partenope* (Iford Opera); *TRYL* (*The Magic Flute*) (Copenhagen Opera Festival); *Klippies, East of Berlin, Monster* (Southwark Playhouse); *Nest* (Vault Festival); *Constellations* (Theatre Municipal De Fontainebleau); *The Prophet* (Gate); *Sex with a Stranger* (Trafalgar Studios); *Elegy for a Lady, The Yalta Game* (Salisbury Playhouse); *Fleabag* (Underbelly/Soho/UK tour); *Lean* (Tristan Bates); *Flashes* (Soho); *Now This Is Not The End, Façade, Eight Songs for a Mad King, Handel Furioso, Sound of a Voice* (Arcola); *Die Fledermaus* (King's Head/OperaUpClose); *Below The Belt* (Pleasance Courtyard/Omnibus); *The Cage Birds* (LAMDA's Linbury Studio); *Who's Afraid of Rachel Roberts* (Torch).

BEN JACOBS | LIGHTING DESIGNER

Ben Jacobs trained at the Royal Central School of Speech and Drama and won the 2018 Off West End Award for Best Lighting Design.

Lighting design credits include: *Bring it On!* (Southwark Playhouse); *Le Morte D'Arthur* (The Scoop); *A Midsummer Night's Dream* (Wilton's Music Hall); *Sister* (Ovalhouse); *Maggie & Pierre, Dolphins & Sharks, The Melting Pot* (Finborough); *Hamlet, Burial at Thebes, Secret Circus* (RCSSD); *Imagine This, Privates on Parade, Carmen 1808, Twang!, HRAitch* (Union); *Edward II, Lord of the Flies* (Greenwich); *Love Me Now* (Tristan Bates); *In Event of Moone Disaster, The State We're In, EleXion* (Theatre503); *People We Didn't Quite Meet, Red, Are We Stronger Than Winston* (The Place); *Cuncrete, Mrs Armitage and the Big Wave* (national tour); *The White Rose, The State of Things, Side By Side By Sondheim, Macbeth* (OFFIE nominated for Best Lighting Design); *Edgar Allen Poe Double Bill, Frankenstein, Wolves of Willoughby Chase* (OFFIE winner for Best Lighting Design); *Adam & Eve* (Jack Studio); *Free Fall* (Pleasance London); *Jamaica Inn, Fanny and Faggot, The Lost Happy Endings* (Tabard); *Macbeth* (Bussey Building); *When the Dove Returns* (Blue Elephant); *Fluxorama* (Clifftown Theatre); *Citizen Puppet* (New Diorama); *Free Fall* (Pleasance); *The Greene Card* (The Space); *Bibs Boats Borders & Bastards* (Cockpit); *Lunatic, The League of Youth* (Theatre N16); *The Last Days of Judas Iscariot* (LESOCO).

Associate Lighting: Project O (Southbank Centre); *Crave* (Prague Quadrennial); *Les Misérables* (Imperial Theatre, Tokyo); *Miss Sarah* (ZOO Venues, Edinburgh); *Legally Blonde* (Watford Palace).

Assistant Lighting: *The Lorax* (The Old Vic); *Out of His Skin* (UK tour); *Finding Joy* (UK tour).

JAC COOPER | SOUND DESIGNER

Jac Cooper trained at the Bristol Old Vic Theatre School. Since then he has been working as a composer and sound designer in the London theatre scene.

Credits include: *Still Here* (Edinburgh Fringe 2016); *All That We Found Here* (Dublin New Theatre); *Snapshot* (Hope, Islington); *Network Diagnostics* (Brighton Fringe 2017); *Nest* (VAULT FestivaL); *Locked Up* (Tristan Bates).

THEATRE 503

Theatre503 is the home of new writers and a launchpad for the artists who bring their words to life. We are pioneers in supporting new writers and a champion of their role in the theatre ecology. We find exceptional playwrights who will define the canon for the next generation. Learning and career development are at the core of what we do. We stage the work of more debut and emerging writers than any other theatre in the country. In the last year alone we staged 70 productions featuring 161 writers from short plays to full runs of superb drama and launching over 1,000 artists in the process. We passionately believe the most important element in a writer's development is to see their work developed through to a full production on stage, performed to the highest professional standard in front of an audience.

Over the last decade many first-time writers have gone on to establish a career in the industry thanks to the support of Theatre503: Tom Morton-Smith (*Oppenheimer*, RSC & West End), Anna Jordan (Bruntwood Prize Winner for *Yen*, Royal Exchange, Royal Court and Broadway), Vinay Patel (writer of the BAFTA-winning *Murdered By My Father*), Katori Hall (*Mountaintop*, 503, West End & Broadway – winner of 503's first Olivier Award) and Jon Brittain (*Rotterdam* – winner of our second Olivier Award in 2017).

Theatre503 Team

Artistic Director	Lisa Spirling
Executive Director	Andrew Shepherd
Producer	Jake Orr
Literary Manager	Steve Harper
Operations Manager	Anna De Freitas
Marketing Coordinator	Rebecca Usher
Technical Manager	Alastair Borland
Literary Associate	Lauretta Barrow
Operations Assistant	Nyanna Bentham-Price
Resident Assistant Producers	Jessica Moncur, Liam McLaughlin, Alex Sikkink, Rhys Newcombe-Jones

Theatre503 Board

Erica Whyman (Chair), Royce Bell (Vice Chair), Chris Campbell, Joachim Fleury, Celine Gagnon, Eleanor Lloyd, Marcus Markou, Geraldine Sharpe-Newton, Jack Tilbury, Roy Williams OBE

Theatre503 Volunteers

Anita Adam Gabay, Emma Anderson, Ane Miren Arriaga, Emily Brearley-Bayliss, Ciaran Chillingworth, Rogerio Correa, Debra Dempster, Abbigale Duncanson, Claire Finn, Beatrice Hollands, Gareth Jones, George Linfield, Emrys Lloyd-Roberts, Ceri Lothian, Berit Moback, Olivia Munk, Christina Murdock, Denitsa Pashova, Annabel Pemberton, Lucy Robson, Kate Roche, Sussan Sanii, Chloe Saunders, Laura Sedgwick, Paul Sockett, Caroline Summers, Aydan Tair, Stephanie Withers.

Our Supporters

We are particularly grateful to Philip and Christine Carne and the long-term support of The Carne Trust for our Playwriting Award and 503Five.

Share The Drama Patrons: Angela Hyde-Courtney, Cas & Philip Donald, Darryl Eales, David Baxter, Erica Whyman, Flow Associates, Geraldine Sharpe-Newton, James Bell, Jill Segal, Kay Ellen Colsover, Nick Hern, Marcus Markou, Marianne Badrichani, Michael North, Mike Morfey, Pam Alexander, Patricia Hamzahee, Robert O'Dowd, Rotha Bell, Sean Winnett.

Theatre Refurbishment: Jack Tilbury, Plann, Dynamis, CharcoalBlue, Stage Solutions, Will Bowen, The Theatres Trust

The Foyle Foundation, Arts Council England Grants for the Arts, The Peter Wolff Foundation (503 Production Fund), The Orseis Trust (503Five), Battersea Power Station Foundation (Right to Write) Barbara Broccoli/EON, M&G Investments (Five-O-Fresh), Nick Hern Books (503 Playwriting Award), Wandsworth Borough Council, The Golsonscott Foundation.

Theatre503 is in receipt of funding from Arts Council England's Catalyst: Evolve fund, match funding every pound raised in new income until July 2019.

Nothing bigger than the truth

Small Truth Theatre is an award-winning company that seeks to create theatre that is collaborative, experiential, detailed and has heart.

Small Truth Theatre is a collective that is proud of its working-class roots and strives to give voice to the seldom heard.

The company specialise in new writing and relish casting a light on the ordinary to discover and celebrate the extraordinary.

Four Small Truths

1. Small Truth Theatre produces shows that discover moments of truth that often go unseen.

2. The company makes work in non-traditional spaces for non-typical theatre audiences – no matter what class, cultural background or how much money you have in your pockets.

3. Small Truth Theatre are known for their down-to-earth, honest approach to making theatre – theatre that is a shared experience in an open, democratic, live, communal space.

4. Making shows as a 'collective' is what Small Truth Theatre does best – all in it together – ensuring we all, actors, creatives and audience, have a good time in the process.

For more information on the company please visit the website
www.smalltruththeatre.com

or follow

  @smalltruthstage

  facebook.com/smalltruththeatre

  instagram.com/smalltruththeatre

Special thank-you to Charlotte Jane Higgins, Martha Brett, Robyn Bennett and all our collaborators past, present and future.

CATERPILLAR

Alison Carr

To Ma and Pa Carr

Characters

CLAIRE, *mid-thirties*
MAEVE, *sixties, Claire's mother*
SIMON, *early twenties, a guest*
JAMIE, *Claire's husband* (*voice only*)
CALLUM, *four, Claire's son* (*voice only*)

Setting

Present day.

A seaside town, a weekend in July.

This text went to press before the end of rehearsals and so may differ slightly from the play as performed.

Scene One

In the sky.

CLAIRE. I launch myself off the pier. The wind fills my ears
and my fingertips brush a cloud as I soar past. It's soft, as
fluffy as the ones your dad painted on your bedroom wall for
when we brought you home and are still there.

I'm propelling forward, still forward, have I made the
jackpot distance? I'm probably not even close, but then –

A gust whips your birthday balloons out of my hand. I watch
them skitter away, brightly coloured dots in the blue. I brace
myself for the plummet, but no.

The wind is now a breeze is now a whisper and I've stopped;
suspended in the sky. The light glistening off the water is
blinding.

I slowly stretch myself out as long as I can go. I feel my
spine crick and uncurl, my shoulders loosen. I hold my head
up high for the first time in…

I point my toes. I hold my fingers like a dancer. Like I think
a dancer might. I'm not really sure.

My body hangs here. My mind is quiet. I breathe the clean
crisp air, in and out, deep and long. I picture my lungs filling
to bursting. I picture you.

I don't know how long this will last. It's already gone on
longer than I dreamed. The drop is coming. But I've done it.
It's done. I jumped.

Scene Two

The front room of a seaside guesthouse. The decor is chintzy, nautical, seaside-y.

Exit off to the hallway, stairs, kitchen, bedrooms, etc.

Saturday. Very early morning.

A lamp is on.

CLAIRE *lies on the settee, asleep. Or maybe passed out.*

A couple of empty bottles of wine and one glass are on the coffee table.

There's a soft knocking on the front door.

Nothing moves.

The knocking gets louder, more insistent.

CLAIRE *stirs. Groans.*

The doorbell rings. It's obnoxiously loud.

CLAIRE *wakes with a jolt. She's not sure where she is for a moment.*

The doorbell rings again.

CLAIRE. Stop it.

But it rings again. She staggers to the door but doesn't open it.

Stop.

SIMON (*outside*). Hello?

CLAIRE. Stop ringing the bell.

SIMON (*outside*). Sorry.

CLAIRE. Who is it?

SIMON (*outside*). Simon.

CLAIRE. Who?

SIMON (*outside*). Simon Logan. I'm booked in for the weekend.

CLAIRE. No you're not.

　What time is it?

SIMON (*outside*). I'm not sure. After one. Have I got the
　wrong place?

　Bay View B&B, 8 Marine Walk –

CLAIRE. All reservations have been cancelled.

SIMON (*outside*). Not mine.

CLAIRE. Yes yours. Everyone's. I sent an email.

SIMON (*outside*). I didn't get one.

CLAIRE. Yeah, I definitely emailed you. I remember. (*She
　doesn't.*)

SIMON (*outside*). Are you Maeve? The only email I've had
　from you is this one confirming my booking.

　He pushes an email printout through the letterbox.

　It's all paid for. Two nights.

　CLAIRE *takes the printout and skims it.*

CLAIRE. Shit.

SIMON (*outside*). What?

CLAIRE. Look, I'm sorry, but we're not taking guests at the
　moment. Circumstances beyond our control.

　Anyway, see, this says check-in between 2 and 8 p.m.

SIMON (*outside*). Yes.

CLAIRE. You're well outside that. Goodnight then.

SIMON (*outside*). Please. Please I've come a really long way.

CLAIRE. . . .

SIMON (*outside*). I'll pay more. I'll pay a late fee. Whatever
　you want.

　Are you still there? Hello?

CLAIRE *is silent, hoping he'll go. All is quiet.*

Then SIMON *kicks the door, making* CLAIRE *jump.*

CLAIRE. Oi, watch it.

SIMON (*outside*). Sorry, I thought you'd... Sorry.

Fuck.

He bangs the door again.

Sorry.

You know when you want so much for everything to be perfect, but then it manages to be the exact opposite of perfect.

CLAIRE. I do, yeah.

SIMON (*outside*). Yeah. Of course it's all gone to shit. Everything I do always does.

I'm sorry. I'll go. I'm sorry.

CLAIRE *opens the door.*

SIMON *stands on the doorstep. He carries an overnight bag.*

Really?

Thank you. Thank you, I am so sorry about all this.

CLAIRE. Hang on.

That late fee.

SIMON. How much?

CLAIRE. Fifty quid. A tenner an hour.

SIMON *pays her. She pockets it.*

ID. You could be anyone.

SIMON. Driver's licence okay?

CLAIRE. Fine.

He retrieves his driver's licence.

SIMON. It's not a very good photo.

CLAIRE. No.

SIMON. My friends say it makes me look like a serial killer.

I'm not, though.

CLAIRE. What?

SIMON. A serial killer.

CLAIRE. No. A serial killer would make more effort to look less like a serial killer.

SIMON. I hadn't thought of it like that.

CLAIRE pockets the licence.

Erm, I –

CLAIRE. Insurance. Stop you robbing us blind. I'll give it back when you go.

SIMON comes in.

They stand awkwardly. Eventually –

SIMON. It's a lovely house.

CLAIRE. You haven't seen any of it.

SIMON. No.

This bit's nice, though. If this is any indication…

Are you alright?

CLAIRE. What?

SIMON. You're bleeding –

He gestures to her T-shirt, it has blood on the hem.

CLAIRE. Shit.

SIMON. Are you okay?

CLAIRE. Fine. It's just some splatter from the last guest who woke me up at 1 a.m.

SIMON *laughs nervously.* CLAIRE *remains straight-faced.*

SIMON. I'm so sorry. Again. I was coming out of the services and this bloke ploughed right into the side of me. He was eating a pasty, didn't see me. No one was hurt but I had to do everything properly, you know. Ring one-oh-one. Get his details, take photos.

CLAIRE. I hope you took a photo of his pasty.

SIMON. I did, yeah. The van's rented and I want my deposit back.

I tried to make the time up but I had to pull over in the next services I was shaking so much. Then the traffic –

CLAIRE. Well you're here now, so you can have the Starfish Room. It's not set up... I mean, it's a bedroom with a bed, but there's no mint on your pillow or anything like that, with your booking being cancelled.

SIMON. Why's it called 'Starfish'?

CLAIRE. Dunno. Cos we're at the seaside.

Up the stairs to the first landing, on the left. It's open and you can lock it from the inside, but Maeve'll have to sort you out with keys tomorrow. All that stuff is her domain.

SIMON. Are you not – ?

CLAIRE. I'm her daughter.

SIMON. Oh.

CLAIRE. The bathroom's on the same landing opposite. There's towels in the airing cupboard.

SIMON. Thanks.

CLAIRE. Anything else you want?

SIMON. I don't think so, no.

CLAIRE. Great.

Last thing, don't come upstairs.

SIMON. Sorry?

CLAIRE. Your room's fine, bathroom, you can come down to the kitchen if you must for a drink, but if I hear you coming up those stairs to the top landing, to my room or Mum's –

SIMON. I wouldn't.

CLAIRE. Good. Don't. I was a teenager in this house, I know all the creaks on that staircase, every squeak that landing makes. Any peep out of you, I've got pepper spray off the internet. It's probably illegal and burning your face off will really fuck up her score on Trip Advisor.

SIMON. You're kidding again.

CLAIRE. No.

SIMON. Okay.

CLAIRE (*deadly serious*). No.

Sleep well, then.

SIMON. Night.

CLAIRE. Night.

Exit SIMON *to the hallway.*

CLAIRE *returns to the settee.*

She drinks the final dregs of wine.

Scene Three

The guesthouse.

Later the same morning.

MAEVE *is in her dressing gown, eating breakfast. Her left arm is tucked into her side – it is very weakened from a stroke.*

Enter SIMON. *He wears jeans and a zipped-up hoodie.*

SIMON. Oh.

    Hello.

MAEVE. Here he is.

SIMON. Morning. I didn't think anyone was up.

    Maeve, is it?

MAEVE. The one and only.

SIMON. Simon.

MAEVE. You're up with the larks.

SIMON. Lots to do. Up and at 'em.

MAEVE. I like it.

    Sleep well?

SIMON. Yes, thank you.

    You?

MAEVE. Great.

SIMON. I didn't wake you, then?

MAEVE. When?

SIMON. Last night. Well, this morning really.

MAEVE. I sleep the sleep of the dead, love. Didn't hear a peep.

SIMON. Good.

MAEVE. Why, what were you doing that was so noisy? And why wasn't I invited?

SIMON. Oh. I was late, my van –

MAEVE. I know. Claire accosted me coming out the bathroom on her way to bed, rambled some tale at me. You turning up regardless –

SIMON. I never got her email.

MAEVE. Course you didn't. Honestly, she had one job.

I wish I'd been up to greet you. I'd usually have nibbles ready, a glass of bubbles.

SIMON. Sounds nice.

MAEVE. It is.

You should have rung, I'd have waited up, got you sorted out.

SIMON. My phone died.

MAEVE. Not your night, was it.

SIMON. No.

MAEVE. I can't have missed you by much. I was up quite late watching a *Die Hard* double-bill.

SIMON. Great.

MAEVE. I can't not watch it.

Do you know it?

SIMON. I've seen it.

MAEVE. Did you know, in that scene where Hans falls out the window, they dropped Alan Rickman before he was expecting it. That's why he looks so surprised.

SIMON. I don't think I've ever watched it right to the end.

MAEVE. Shall I see when it's next on?

SIMON. It's fine.

MAEVE. Your loss, love.

SIMON. Yes.

MAEVE. Now. Breakfast. I'm afraid there's not the usual selection in with not expecting you. There's some Shreddies, there might be a couple of yogurts left. There's toast if you want toast. The bread's that 50/50 kind so if you like white it's white, if you like brown it's brown.

Let me have a hunt around, put it out for you like a buffet.

SIMON. There's no need, I can manage.

MAEVE. You're a guest, you shouldn't have to 'manage'.

Here, let me –

She gets up. She's unsteady and bumps into the edge of the coffee table. It hurts.

SIMON. You okay?

MAEVE. Fine.

SIMON. Honestly, I can get it myself. Just point me in the right direction.

MAEVE. Through the door, turn left to the kitchen. If nothing grabs you I'll send Claire to the shop.

SIMON. I'll be fine.

Can I get you another coffee?

MAEVE. Your mum raised you right, didn't she. Another in there would be grand.

SIMON. No problem.

MAEVE. And there's keys on the kitchen table for you.

SIMON takes her mug. He goes to leave.

Enter CLAIRE. She is dressed for the day apart from bare feet. She has a glass of water and knocks back a couple of aspirin.

Morning.

CLAIRE. Everyone's up early.

SIMON. Yes.

CLAIRE (*to* MAEVE). I thought you'd be sleeping in after your late night watching Bruce run around in his sweaty vest.

MAEVE. I had a lovely sleep. Fully refreshed and raring to go.

CLAIRE. Glad one of us is.

MAEVE. I was just saying, wasn't I, what a heavy sleeper I am.

Her dad used to worry I had actually passed on. When we were first married I was forever waking up to him holding a mirror under my nose to check if I was still breathing.

CLAIRE. Probably wishful thinking.

Are my trainers in here? I can't find them.

MAEVE. When you've got them, nip to the shops and get some breakfast things in, will you.

CLAIRE. We've got breakfast things in.

MAEVE (*to* SIMON). What would you like, love?

SIMON. I'll be fine with toast.

MAEVE. No. That's no fun. Toast. Not when you're on your holidays.

Claire, go out and get the doings for a fry-up.

Bacon, sausage, fried bread. How does that sound?

SIMON. Fantastic.

MAEVE. You'll tell your grandkids about my fried bread, won't he.

CLAIRE. You can't do a fry-up.

MAEVE. Of course I can.

CLAIRE. Hardly.

MAEVE. Look, the lad's salivating at the thought.

CLAIRE. You can't.

MAEVE. I can.

CLAIRE. One handed?

MAEVE (*burst of anger*). Yes. For fuck's sake.

Sorry.

I'm sorry.

SIMON. That's okay.

CLAIRE. I wish it was the stroke that's made her unhinged, but it's always been thus.

MAEVE. Do you want to tell him about my thrush too?

SIMON. I'm probably best staying off the fry-ups.

MAEVE. There's not a pick on you.

Unless Claire wants to cook it?

CLAIRE. No thank you.

Are you sure you haven't moved them?

MAEVE. What?

CLAIRE. My trainers.

MAEVE. Try the utility room.

CLAIRE. So you have moved them.

MAEVE. No. But it's like a black hole, things end up in there.

CLAIRE *goes to exit*.

Where are you off to so early, anyway?

CLAIRE. Mick's. I said I'd help out.

MAEVE. Again?

CLAIRE. The new girl is still off sick. It's coming out of both ends and not stopping.

MAEVE. But you're heading home today.

CLAIRE. Yes. Later.

MAEVE. What time's Callum's party?

CLAIRE. There's ages. Mick just needs me for the morning rush. He's expecting loads of losers turning up for this thing.

MAEVE. It's her son's birthday.

SIMON. Lovely.

CLAIRE. Yeah, okay, he doesn't give a shit.

SIMON. I do.

CLAIRE. Why? No you don't.

Exit CLAIRE *to the hallway.*

MAEVE. Sorry about her, customer service isn't her strong point.

SIMON. That's okay.

MAEVE. I've done courses.

SIMON. Have you?

MAEVE. I'm verified, certified, health and safety aware, rated five out of five for food hygiene, there's a first-aid kit and fire extinguisher on every landing.

SIMON. Very reassuring.

MAEVE. It's usually me at the helm, hostess with the mostess, but, well… (*Her arm.*)

SIMON. Right.

MAEVE. It's my left, actually. Boom boom.

SIMON. Yes. Sorry.

MAEVE. Me too, lad. Me too. A hotelier without guests is a terrible thing.

But I'm not sans guests any more, am I.

SIMON. No.

MAEVE. No. I've got you. You slipped through the cracks.

Word to the wise, that front door can be a bit tricky but don't be gentle with it, it just needs a good shove.

SIMON. Okay.

MAEVE. Don't we all.

Sit.

SIMON *perches*.

So. Are you here to watch the competition?

SIMON. I'm taking part.

MAEVE. Really?

SIMON. Yes.

MAEVE. Oh.

SIMON. What?

MAEVE. No, just, you don't look the type.

SIMON. What's 'the type'?

MAEVE. I don't know.

What's your category?

SIMON. Eagle.

MAEVE. What time's your slot?

SIMON. Quarter to three.

MAEVE. Today?

SIMON. Yes.

MAEVE. Great. Well. Good luck.

SIMON. Thanks.

CLAIRE *bustles in, catches the tail-end of previous*.

CLAIRE. Good luck with what?

MAEVE. Simon's here for the Birdman competition. He's taking part.

SIMON. I'm one of those 'losers' you mentioned.

CLAIRE. They're not in the utility room.

MAEVE. Just wear another pair of shoes.

CLAIRE. I didn't bring another pair of shoes with me.

MAEVE. Well that's just stupid.

CLAIRE. I'm going to be late

Exit CLAIRE *to the hallway.*

MAEVE (*calling after her*). If that Mick's got a problem, tell him he's lucky to have you.

(*To* SIMON.) He keeps hauling her in there, it's ridiculous. The Seashell Café it's called. Along the promenade, there. That's not her job job. She's just here on a visit. She's a finance officer at a lovely school, posh. Lots of responsibility.

SIMON. Great.

MAEVE. Not slinging soggy toasties in some tacky café with plastic tablecloths.

SIMON. No.

MAEVE. She's off for the summer holidays now, of course. Another perk.

SIMON. Nice.

MAEVE. What is it you do?

SIMON. I'm self-employed

MAEVE. Very entrepreneurial. Doing what?

SIMON. I'm a food courier.

MAEVE. A delivery boy?

SIMON. No.

Enter CLAIRE. *She carries her bag, coat and trainers.*

CLAIRE. Found them.

MAEVE. Where were they?

CLAIRE. One was in the wardrobe. The other in the laundry basket.

MAEVE. Obviously.

SIMON. Do you take milk and sugar?

MAEVE. A splash of milk.

CLAIRE. Skimmed, red top.

MAEVE. And two sugars.

CLAIRE. One sugar.

MAEVE. One and a half sugars.

CLAIRE. One sugar.

MAEVE. Heaped.

CLAIRE. In no way heaped.

SIMON. Okay.

MAEVE. Have we met?

SIMON. I don't think so.

MAEVE. Are you sure? Just then, when you turned your head, I thought, 'I've seen that face.' And I make it my business to remember handsome faces.

CLAIRE. Yeah, alright, Liz Taylor. Leave the young man alone.

MAEVE. Only Liz's last husband was younger than her, actually.

CLAIRE (*to* SIMON). Keys – don't lose them.

MAEVE. Come and go as you please.

CLAIRE. The front door – sometimes it plays up, but just shove it.

SIMON. Yes, Maeve was saying.

CLAIRE. Mavis.

MAEVE. Maeve.

CLAIRE. She thinks Maeve sounds exotic. Lip gloss and feathers, not Werther's Originals and a stairlift.

MAEVE. We're a long way off that yet.

CLAIRE. You keep telling yourself that.

It's better than Claire, I suppose.

MAEVE. Claire is a nice name, solid.

SIMON. I had a guinea pig growing up called Claire.

CLAIRE. Well there we are, a pig for a namesake.

SIMON. No. She won competitions.

MAEVE. Doing what?

SIMON. My mum breeds them. Guinea pigs. Claire was the star.

CLAIRE (*to* MAEVE). Did you hear that, a star.

MAEVE. I heard.

CLAIRE. Have a think what you'll want for lunch. Or do you want something brought from the café?

MAEVE. You'll be gone by lunchtime, won't you?

CLAIRE. I'll do your lunch then go.

MAEVE. There's no need.

CLAIRE *puts her coat on.*

I don't think you'll need a coat, it's going to be glorious.

CLAIRE. I'll see you later.

Exit CLAIRE *outside* (*with her coat on*).

MAEVE. And then there were two.

SIMON. Yes.

MAEVE. Help yourself to whatever you can find.

SIMON. Thanks.

Exit SIMON *to the kitchen.*

Scene Four

Outside. A path along the promenade.

Later.

SIMON *sits on a bench. He has one shoe and sock off. His hoodie is also off, underneath he wears a T-shirt that reads 'Emmie's Wish'.*

He is writing in a notebook.

Enter CLAIRE. *She has a frilly pinny on. No coat. Sleeves rolled up.*

She notices him and calls over –

CLAIRE. Alright?

Gorgeous, isn't it. The sun on your face. It makes such a difference.

SIMON *doesn't respond. He has finished writing in his notebook, has ripped the page out and is folding it into a paper aeroplane.*

I thought there'd be more people, they've got enough barriers up.

What time is it? (*Checks her phone.*) …Is that all? This is what happens when you have an early start. Mick had us open the café a whole extra hour earlier than normal. There's been about three people in so far.

CLAIRE *considers his bare foot.*

Is this a thing, is it? This?

One bare foot. Is it a thing for this competition, some code amongst you jumpers? Is it like the Masons?

She watches him with the paper plane.

I don't think that's going to take you very far.

He ignores her. CLAIRE *gives up on him. She retrieves a packet of cigarettes from her pinny pocket. She hunts for a lighter.*

Have you got a light?

SIMON....

CLAIRE. Oi. Stop being an ignorant prick.

SIMON. I don't smoke.

CLAIRE. No one fucking smokes any more.

She shoves the cigarette back in the packet and goes to leave.

SIMON. Flyer.

CLAIRE. Eh?

SIMON. Participants are called flyers, not jumpers.

We're not jumping, we're flying. Trying to.

CLAIRE. I'll remember that for next time I'm talking to a pedant.

SIMON. I think my foot might be broken.

CLAIRE. What did you do to it?

SIMON. I was kicking my van.

CLAIRE. Okay.

Is it swollen? Take off your other shoe, we can compare.

She sits next to him. He turns himself away from her.

Can I do one? (*Re: paper plane.*)

SIMON. It's not for fun.

CLAIRE. But you look like you're having such a whale of
a time.

If not for fun, then why?

SIMON. You write down what's making you angry or sad or
scared and throw it into the wind. Watch your fears fly away.

CLAIRE. Right.

Does it work?

SIMON. It's the process, isn't it. The psychology.

CLAIRE. I get that. It's just... it all sounds – what's the word?
Like bullshit.

SIMON....

CLAIRE. What does yours say?

SIMON. It's private.

CLAIRE. Fine.

SIMON. I'll need to get my stuff but I'll post the keys through the letterbox, or leave them with Maeve if she's in.

CLAIRE. You're leaving?

SIMON. Yes.

CLAIRE. What about the competition?

SIMON. I'm not doing it.

CLAIRE. Why not?

SIMON. My wings are fucked.

CLAIRE. What?

SIMON. My glider. For the competition.

I went along to the van this morning and... I knew it was knocked about last night but I didn't realise how badly.

The frame's twisted, bits have snapped off. There's a hole in it, for Christ's sake.

CLAIRE. Shit.

SIMON. If that bastard had just looked up from his Steak Bake.

CLAIRE. Can you patch it up?

SIMON. If I wanted to do a half-arsed job then, yeah, of course, just patch it up.

Who cares. Who wants to do anything properly.

CLAIRE. Alright.

SIMON. There's no time, anyway.

Fuck. I've let her down. Again.

CLAIRE. Who?

SIMON. I can just picture her face. The eyebrow raised, arms folded.

CLAIRE. It's not your fault, she'll understand.

SIMON. How do you know?

CLAIRE. I'm just trying to make you feel better.

SIMON. Well you're not.

CLAIRE. Can't she come and help you mend it, if it's so important?

SIMON. No.

CLAIRE. Can't be that big of a deal then, can it. If she can't be bothered to get off her arse –

SIMON. She's dead.

CLAIRE. Oh.

SIMON. Yeah. (*Starts to cry.*)

CLAIRE*'s uncomfortable. She moves away, looks out.*

CLAIRE. One of the first things they built on the pier was a souvenir shop, you know. In the 1800s. Then a pavilion. It all got washed away. A storm. We did a school project on it. The decking between the pavilion and the shore, gone. They sold postcards of views of the wreckage and I remember thinking 'That's the kind of thing Mum would do', you know. Look for a way to turn a profit even in misfortune. It's jinxed, I think. The pier. Cos it burned down as well. And during the war they blew a massive hole in it.

Pause.

Do I need to keep going, or have you stopped crying?

SIMON. Yes.

CLAIRE. Yes keep going, or yes you've stopped?

SIMON. I've stopped.

SIMON *stands and approaches her, looking out.*

Sorry.

CLAIRE. Forget it.

SIMON. You'll be glad of this quiet time soon. It'll busy up.

CLAIRE. Yeah?

SIMON. Last year – crazy. Emmie loved it, though.

The bustle, the people, the noise.

CLAIRE. Is that who died? Emmie?

SIMON. Yes.

CLAIRE. That explains your T-shirt, then. I thought it was
some band I'd never heard of.

So what was 'Emmie's Wish'?

SIMON. That I came back here this year and flew. She made me
promise.

CLAIRE. This is my first time here when the competition's
been on. I feel like I'm hunkering down for battle.

SIMON. It's all pretty good-natured.

CLAIRE. Were you jumpi– flying or watching last year?

SIMON. Just watching.

Emmie thought it was brilliant, all these people taking leaps
of faith into the sea.

CLAIRE. 'Brilliant' is one word for it.

SIMON. The contraptions they come up with. There's fancy
dress, bands, stalls, music – you'll love it.

CLAIRE. If you say so.

SIMON. Emmie wanted us to dress up as Peter Pan and Tinker
Bell, flying off together to Never Neverland.

CLAIRE. Sounds nauseating.

Are you going to throw that thing or what?

He throws the paper plane. It's not impressive.

Feel better?

SIMON. I never could make them very well. Emmie's would do loop-de-loops.

CLAIRE. Can't you just stay and watch? Be part of it that way?

SIMON. I've raised money, got sponsors. I've got fifty of these T-shirts in the van.

Do you want one?

CLAIRE. No thanks.

SIMON. It was her last request that I fly.

CLAIRE. I'm sorry.

SIMON. Me too.

CLAIRE. I better get back or Mick'll come looking.

See you.

SIMON. Bye.

CLAIRE. There's always next year. It's not like she'll know.

SIMON. I'll know.

CLAIRE. Still.

Exit CLAIRE.

Scene Five

The guesthouse.

Midday.

A small wheelie suitcase is in the corner.

MAEVE *is still in her dressing gown and nightie.*

MAEVE *has a foot peddler up on the coffee table that she is revolving with her hands. She is struggling with her left arm but she persists.*

A half-eaten sandwich is also on the table, and a mug of coffee.

Enter CLAIRE *from outside.*

MAEVE. Have you seen the time? I've been ringing you.

CLAIRE. I left my phone upstairs.

MAEVE. You need to get going.

CLAIRE. It's fine.

MAEVE. You'll never be back for one.

CLAIRE. I don't need to be. Jamie's taking them to the soft play and I'll see them back at the house later for candles and cake.

MAEVE. Don't you want to go to the soft play?

CLAIRE. Not really.

MAEVE. It's his birthday.

CLAIRE. And I'll be there.

MAEVE. I've packed your stuff in your case.

CLAIRE. What?

MAEVE. There. (*The suitcase.*)

CLAIRE. Anyone'd think you want to see the back of me.

MAEVE. No. I was being helpful.

CLAIRE. You shouldn't be carrying this downstairs.

MAEVE. I bounced it down on the wheels. It's not exactly heavy.

CLAIRE. I travel light, it's a skill.

MAEVE. I don't know if you want to do a once around, check you've got everything.

CLAIRE. Let me catch my breath, will you.

I can't just hop in the car, I'm frazzled.

CLAIRE *flops down next to her.*

She helps herself to a bite of sandwich.

MAEVE. I've done you one for the journey, it's in the fridge.

CLAIRE. What's that? (*Re: the peddler.*)

MAEVE. It's for building up strength.

CLAIRE. Where did you get it from?

MAEVE. I ordered it online.

CLAIRE. You don't seem to be making a very good job of it.

MAEVE. I am. Compare this to where I was a month ago, a week ago even. I'm a bloody miracle.

CLAIRE *retrieves an envelope of cash from her bag.*

Look at you, flashy. Is that off Mick?

CLAIRE. Yes.

MAEVE. Under the table, sly git.

I hope he paid you double, getting him out of a jam.

CLAIRE. I enjoy it. Up on my feet, not rotting behind some desk.

That's for you.

MAEVE. You don't need to.

CLAIRE. Yes. It's the shifts I've done, plus tips. I don't get many tips.

MAEVE. Quelle surprise.

CLAIRE. For my bed and board.

MAEVE. I don't want it.

CLAIRE. You're obviously losing money not having guests.
It's not much but –

MAEVE. No.

CLAIRE. Angie's been helping you out, let me.

MAEVE (*taking the money*). Thank you.

CLAIRE. Oh, and this –

CLAIRE *pulls* SIMON*'s fifty quid from her jeans pocket*.

MAEVE. What's this from?

CLAIRE. I charged Simon a late check-in fee.

MAEVE. There's no such thing.

CLAIRE. He didn't know that.

MAEVE. Fifty quid.

You keep it.

CLAIRE. No.

MAEVE. You earned it. Have you ever thought of going into
the hotelier business?

CLAIRE. We'll split it.

MAEVE. Poor sod, I already stung him with a higher rate with
it being this weekend.

CLAIRE *puts thirty quid on the table, pockets the other
twenty.*

CLAIRE. Is there a pot of coffee on?

MAEVE. Yes. It might be a bit stale.

CLAIRE. Do you want a top-up?

MAEVE. If there's enough.

Exit CLAIRE *to the kitchen with* MAEVE*'s mug.*

MAEVE *returns to the peddler. Her bad arm keeps falling off the pedal. She pushes the machine away, frustrated.*

CLAIRE *returns with the coffees.*

CLAIRE. It's chaos out there. I blinked and it went from deserted to chock-a-block.

MAEVE. It takes over.

CLAIRE. The café is heaving. The beach is rammed. There's no parking.

MAEVE. Have you watched any?

CLAIRE. I saw a couple dressed as penguins as I walked over. They waddled about and then plopped in to the water.

MAEVE. The fun charity ones are the best. Some take it far too seriously.

CLAIRE. I didn't think penguins could fly.

MAEVE. That's the joke, isn't it.

CLAIRE. Is there a prize?

MAEVE. Twenty-five grand.

CLAIRE. Fuck off.

MAEVE. I know. Ten years ago when it started, two hundred quid and a free drink in the pub. Now...

CLAIRE. I saw all the branding.

MAEVE. Peanuts to them, isn't it.

CLAIRE. So they swan in, find a spare twenty grand for people dressing up stupid and jumping off the pier, then piss off again?

MAEVE. Yes.

CLAIRE. Disgusting.

MAEVE. It brings in the tourists.

CLAIRE. For two days of the year.

MAEVE. Better than nothing.

CLAIRE. I suppose.

MAEVE. There's three categories: 'Cayley' for self-designed, self-built craft; 'Eagle' for modified hang-gliders and things like that; and then the Fun Flyers in fancy dress.

CLAIRE. So who wins the money?

MAEVE. If they fly more than a hundred metres from the first two categories, they get the jackpot.

The funniest ones, the best costumes, they get a few hundred for first, second and third.

CLAIRE. Aren't you the expert.

MAEVE. I was a steward last year.

And this weather, it'll be even busier. Last year it rained rods.

CLAIRE. I can imagine you strutting about in a high-viz vest.

MAEVE. And a walkie-talkie.

CLAIRE. Dear God. 'This is Charlie Echo to Foxtrot Alpha, are you receiving me, over?'

MAEVE. 'That's a big 10-4 to the affirmative, over and out.'

CLAIRE. Would you do it?

MAEVE. Jump?

CLAIRE. Fly. Get the lingo.

MAEVE. I considered it.

CLAIRE. Seriously?

MAEVE. Why not? But. (*Re: her arm, her stroke*.)

CLAIRE. Next year. I can see you dressed as a penguin.

MAEVE. A parrot, please. Something beautiful. I'm not dumpy enough to be a penguin.

CLAIRE. You should get out there, have a watch.

MAEVE. I'll mooch over in a bit.

CLAIRE. Mick said they're putting a big film screen up.

MAEVE. On the beach?

CLAIRE. Yeah. Deckchairs to watch.

I got you a leaflet with what they're showing.

MAEVE. Thanks.

CLAIRE *retrieves the leaflet.* MAEVE *flicks through.*

CLAIRE. Look at you, still in your nightie in the afternoon.

MAEVE. I'm having a leisurely morning, it's allowed.

CLAIRE. Cover this up.

MAEVE. It's a Marksies nightdress, not crotchless panties.

CLAIRE. That's not the point though, is it. It's not very professional.

MAEVE. There's only you here, I didn't realise that warranted a suit and tie.

CLAIRE. You have a guest.

MAEVE. Not any more. He left about half an hour ago. He lugged his bag and his miserable face past me before spluttering off in that van of his.

CLAIRE. Right.

MAEVE. I remembered where I saw him from.

Yesterday's paper. It's on the side there.

CLAIRE *retrieves the local newspaper.*

A few pages in. Towards the middle.

CLAIRE. Where?

MAEVE. Give it here. Today's hasn't come yet. It gets later and later.

I wanted something to read on the lav, and there he was.

CLAIRE. He's not a murderer on the run, is he?

MAEVE. Something about someone being dead – his sister?

> Here it is. See.

> CLAIRE *reads*.

CLAIRE. His girlfriend. He was telling me about her.

MAEVE. Creepy if you ask me.

CLAIRE. Why?

MAEVE. Carrying her ashes around.

CLAIRE. Where does it say that?

MAEVE. I don't know.

CLAIRE. Look, it says he's got a poem that she wrote for him before she died, not her ashes.

> He was going to jump with the poem, and throw it into the water folded into a paper plane.

MAEVE. Why?

CLAIRE. He promised her.

MAEVE. Look at you, all misty-eyed.

CLAIRE. Hardly.

MAEVE. You'll be back in Jamie's arms soon enough.

CLAIRE. Do you have a vacancies board or something? I can put it in the window, there'll definitely be a taker, the hordes out there.

MAEVE. I don't think so.

CLAIRE. You liked having a guest. You were on fine form this morning. Chatting him up.

MAEVE. I'm tired. You'll be gone.

CLAIRE. I can stay.

MAEVE. No.

CLAIRE. If you're not feeling a hundred per cent. That's the whole point of me being here.

MAEVE. You're going, you've been here long enough.

CLAIRE. You do look quite pale.

MAEVE. I'm always pale. Pale and interesting.

CLAIRE. Mum.

MAEVE. Claire.

CLAIRE. A couple more days –

MAEVE. No need.

CLAIRE. Yes but –

MAEVE. You need to get back. Jamie'll be desperate, minding Cal on his own all this time.

CLAIRE. He's not 'minding' him. He's not doing me a favour. He's his dad.

MAEVE. Still. You've been away from him too long as it is. Beautiful boy.

CLAIRE. Two weeks.

MAEVE. Two and a half.

CLAIRE. Callum won't have even noticed.

MAEVE. Why would you say that?

CLAIRE. He's so young.

MAEVE. Of course he's noticed.

What have you got him for his birthday? Did you get him something from here?

CLAIRE. No. Jamie's getting it.

MAEVE. What is it?

CLAIRE. It's a… Lego. Like a starter-kit.

MAEVE. Send me photos of him opening it. And of the party.

CLAIRE. I will.

MAEVE. I got him a little gardener set. There's a trowel and a watering can.

It'll get him outside.

CLAIRE. He's outside plenty.

MAEVE. Well more won't hurt. Childhood obesity is a thing now.

CLAIRE. He's three.

MAEVE. Four. He's growing up so fast.

CLAIRE. Yes.

MAEVE. I've had it delivered straight to you rather than here, save you carting it back.

CLAIRE. Why don't you come back with me? You can watch him open it live.

MAEVE. Best not, eh.

CLAIRE. You'll get to see him. You can tell him to his face how fat he's looking.

MAEVE. Jamie'll want you to himself, he won't want me hanging about.

CLAIRE. Yes he will. He likes you, God help him.

A couple of days away, change of scenery. A day even, I'll run you back.

MAEVE. I don't think so.

CLAIRE. You stayed with Angie for nearly two months. You're desperate to be away from me after a fortnight.

MAEVE. No. A totally different thing. I was fresh out of hospital then, getting back on my feet. It took time.

Plus, Angie wasn't being pulled this way and that.

CLAIRE. Neither am I. Jamie's fine with me being here, as long as it takes.

MAEVE. I'll be absolutely grand on my tod. It has to happen eventually.

CLAIRE. You'll try and do too much too soon, though.

MAEVE. No I won't. I've learnt my lesson on that score.

Yes?

Yeah?

CLAIRE (*sharp.*) Yes, okay, I just said.

(*Re: the coffee.*) I'm going to make a fresh pot, this is vile.

MAEVE. You need to get going.

CLAIRE *exits to the kitchen.*

The landline telephone rings. MAEVE *picks it up.*

Hello?

Hello, you, were your ears burning?

I'm great. Yes. A hundred per cent. Back on my feet, raring to go.

Everything okay with you? Great. And how's that grandson of mine?

He never did. Cheeky monkey. She is, yes. She's just in the kitchen, one sec.

(*Calling off.*) Claire.

Is he excited for his party?

I bet.

(*Calling off.*) Claire!

Take lots of photos, won't you. I've asked Claire but she never does.

Is that him? Is he there? Put him on.

(*Calling off.*) Claire!

Hello, birthday boy, it's Nana. Hello. You're a big boy now aren't you. How old are you?

Enter CLAIRE.

CLAIRE. What? Stop bellowing.

MAEVE. It's Callum.

MAEVE *puts the phone on speakerphone*.

You're four, aren't you.

CALLUM (*voice*). Yes.

MAEVE. Four today.

CALLUM (*voice*). Yes.

MAEVE. Are you excited for your party?

CALLUM (*voice*). Yes.

MAEVE. Will there be jelly and ice cream and cake?

CALLUM (*voice*). A caterpillar cake.

MAEVE. A caterpillar cake, wow. That sounds amazing.

CALLUM (*voice*). Yes.

MAEVE. Your mum's here. Say hello to Mummy. Cal? Callum?

JAMIE (*voice*). He's gone. He's bouncing off the walls already. Is Claire there?

CLAIRE *takes the phone, but it's still on speaker.*

CLAIRE. Hi.

JAMIE (*voice*). Why aren't you answering your mobile?

CLAIRE. Hang on, you're still on speaker.

JAMIE (*voice*). I've been ringing and texting.

CLAIRE. I lost my mobile.

(*To* MAEVE.) Which button is it?

JAMIE (*voice*). Why aren't you home yet?

CLAIRE. Just wait, can you. Hang on –

She gets the phone off speaker.

Yeah, okay, I know.

I know I should.

I don't know.

CLAIRE *exits to the hallway, closing the door behind her.*
MAEVE *hovers by the door. Occasionally* CLAIRE*'s raised*
voice can be heard, but we can't make out the words.
Suddenly, CLAIRE *is right outside the door –*

(*Off, loud.*) Fine, great, do what you like.

Enter CLAIRE.

Why did you tell him I was still here?

MAEVE. Cos you are.

You said he was fine with it, if I'd known…

CLAIRE. Yeah, well. You should keep your mouth shut.

MAEVE. Is everything okay?

CLAIRE. Yes.

MAEVE. Callum?

CLAIRE. What about him?

MAEVE. He's okay?

CLAIRE. You spoke to him. Did he sound okay?

MAEVE. Yes.

CLAIRE. Right then.

You've made quite a mess in there.

MAEVE. What?

CLAIRE. In the kitchen. Happy enough to make the food to
shove down your neck, but not so hot on tidying up after
yourself. That's for me to do, is it?

MAEVE. No.

CLAIRE. See, this is why I don't want to leave you. You'll let
things slide. Here too, you can't even feed yourself without
making a mess.

MAEVE. I'll clear up in a sec.

CLAIRE. Do it now.

Now.

MAEVE *tries to pick up the few sandwich crumbs off the coffee table.* CLAIRE *watches.*

Useless.

MAEVE. I can do it.

CLAIRE. Leave it. Leave it.

CLAIRE *grabs* MAEVE*'s bad arm and wrenches her out of the way. She's not gentle.*

A beat. A moment. Will this escalate or defuse?

A decision.

CLAIRE *pulls on her coat, retrieves her bag and her wheelie suitcase.*

Exit CLAIRE *outside.*

Scene Six

The guesthouse.

Early evening.

The room is dominated by SIMON*'s homemade hang-glider. It is badly damaged, the frame is broken, the wing fabric is torn.*

MAEVE *surveys the scene. She pokes a piece of the frame with her foot and it falls away.*

Keys in the front door. MAEVE *darts away.*

Enter SIMON *from outside.*

He has a carrier bag of provisions and a handful of children's seaside fishing nets.

He sees MAEVE *frowning at the glider –*

SIMON. Is it still okay? Now you've seen it.

MAEVE. It's big.

SIMON. I said it was big.

MAEVE. You said it was quite big.

SIMON. If it's too much, if you want me to move it.

MAEVE. Yeah, move it.

SIMON. Oh.

Okay.

MAEVE. I'm joshing you, lad. I said you could fix it up in here, you can.

SIMON. Thank you.

MAEVE. If anything gets knocked, you pay for it.

SIMON. Of course.

MAEVE. You really made all this yourself?

SIMON. Yes.

MAEVE. From scratch?

SIMON. Yes.

MAEVE. Where do you even start?

SIMON. PVC pipes for the frame, parachute fabric, some glue, some thread, done.

MAEVE. I feel like it should be more complicated than that.

SIMON. It's as complicated as you make it.

MAEVE. And what's your schtick?

SIMON. Sorry?

MAEVE. Your theme, your costume?

SIMON. Oh. It's a surprise. A local fancy-dress shop, they read about me and… well, you'll see.

MAEVE. Intriguing.

SIMON. Yes.

MAEVE. Well. Good luck.

SIMON. I'll need it.

MAEVE. Yes.

Pause.

SIMON. Did Claire get off okay, to her party?

MAEVE. Yes.

SIMON. Good. I saw her earlier and...

When you next speak to her, will you thank her for me?

MAEVE. For what?

SIMON. I got a bit upset, she tried to help.

MAEVE. Right.

MAEVE *retrieves her coat and handbag.*

SIMON. I'm not driving you out?

MAEVE. Well...

SIMON. Oh shit. No, really. Let me move this, get the telly back over here –

MAEVE. Is that all you think I'm good for? Sitting here watching the telly?

SIMON. Of course not. I didn't mean –

MAEVE. I'm going to watch *Titanic*.

SIMON. Okay.

MAEVE. They've put a big screen up on the beach. It'll be lovely down there on an evening like this.

SIMON. I bet.

MAEVE. Where do you stand on whether Jack could have fitted on the door?

SIMON. Sorry?

MAEVE. Forget it.

MAEVE *goes to exit*.

SIMON. Before you go, did you get a chance to have a look
for –

MAEVE. Yes, sorry. One driver's licence. (*Retrieves it*.)

She didn't take it home, she'd put it in the bedside drawer.

SIMON. Thanks.

MAEVE. How long have you got to get it to them?

SIMON. Seven days. The officer was very understanding, once
I explained. He said he'd read about me in the newspaper.

MAEVE. That's where I saw you. When I asked would I know
you.

SIMON. In the paper?

MAEVE. Yes. You should have mentioned we had a celebrity in
our midst.

SIMON. Well, I wouldn't go that far. (*He would*.)

MAEVE. No.

Condolences about your girlfriend.

SIMON. Thank you.

MAEVE. I used to have these guests, Craig and Des. Lovely
couple, came the same two weeks every year. Des died, very
sad, and the first year Craig came back without him he used
to text him every night with what he'd done that day – went
to the beach, played the slots, had a Coke float – he said it
kept him feeling connected to Des, you know.

SIMON. I can understand that.

MAEVE. The last day of his trip, he got a reply. Des's name
flashed on to the screen, 'Who dis?' Craig nearly had a heart
attack.

SIMON. Somebody playing a joke?

MAEVE. No. The phone company had reassigned Des's number.

SIMON. Bloody hell.

MAEVE. Yup.

That was that.

Silence.

Was Claire okay?

SIMON. Sorry?

MAEVE. When you spoke to her earlier. Was she alright?

SIMON. Fine.

MAEVE. She wasn't anxious or…?

SIMON. I don't really have anything to compare it to. I don't know how she usually is.

MAEVE. Did she say anything or…

SIMON. About what?

MAEVE. Anything.

SIMON. No.

MAEVE. No.

Okay.

If you go out, remember to pull the door.

SIMON. Will do.

Enjoy the film.

MAEVE. I will.

SIMON. Bit of a sick choice, isn't it. About people drowning. Considering.

MAEVE. Suppose.

Kate Winslet nearly drowned during filming, you know.

SIMON. Really.

MAEVE. I read about it. It said there's a 'break point', when the brain makes us take a breath even if we're underwater. Eighty-seven seconds. We can last eighty-seven seconds, then the brain triggers, breath, our lungs fill with water, drowned.

SIMON (*under his breath*). Jesus Christ.

MAEVE. I'll leave you to it.

See you later.

MAEVE pauses in the doorway. Resolve.

Exit MAEVE outside.

SIMON retrieves some bottles of beer from his carrier bag. He drinks. He lays out what he needs and gets to work.

Keys in the door. Enter CLAIRE from outside.

She has cake in her hair.

SIMON. Hi.

CLAIRE. Where's she gone?

SIMON. What?

CLAIRE. Mavis? To the shop, to the post box? How long have I got?

SIMON. She's gone to watch a film on the beach.

CLAIRE. Oh. Really?

Good. Great.

SIMON. I thought you'd gone home.

CLAIRE. I could say the same about you.

Exit CLAIRE to the hallway.

SIMON hovers. Picks about the glider.

Enter CLAIRE.

That's better. I thought my bladder was going to explode.

Can that happen?

SIMON. I imagine you'd just wet yourself before you actually exploded.

CLAIRE. Yeah.

I've been sat in the car willing her to go out.

SIMON. Why didn't you just come in?

CLAIRE. I didn't want her to see me.

SIMON. Go to the toilets at the pub?

CLAIRE. I didn't want anyone to see me. They'd report back.

SIMON. There's a load of portaloos by the beach.

CLAIRE. Yeah alright Piss Master General.

SIMON. Sorry.

CLAIRE (*re: the beer*). Have you got any more of those?

SIMON. Sure.

He passes her a beer. They drink. She gulps hers down.

CLAIRE. You're back, then.

SIMON. Yes.

CLAIRE. What changed your mind?

SIMON. You still had my driver's licence.

CLAIRE. Shit, yes.

SIMON. The van's got a broken tail light. I got pulled over.

CLAIRE. That thing's nothing but trouble

SIMON. Tell me about it.

I went to give my licence to the officer, realised I hadn't gotten it back off you.

CLAIRE. It's upstairs.

SIMON. Yeah, Maeve got it for me.

CLAIRE. You're still here, though. And that – (*The glider.*)

You could have just got your licence and gone.

SIMON. I think it was Emmie.

CLAIRE. What?

SIMON. Moving the universe so I had to come back.

CLAIRE. She can move the universe, wow.

SIMON. Putting obstacles in my way, making me realise I *need* to do this. That it might not be easy, but I have to.

What about you? What happened to the birthday party?

CLAIRE. The universe moved and I left.

CLAIRE *drinks*.

I saw a Del Boy and Rodney jump off the pier earlier in a cardboard Trotters van and this is your effort.

A boring old hand-glider.

SIMON. Hang.

CLAIRE. What?

SIMON. *Hang*-glider.

CLAIRE. That's what I said. Hand-glider.

SIMON. Hang. With a 'g'. As in 'hang' off it. Not 'hand' as in… hand.

CLAIRE. Hang?

SIMON. Yes.

CLAIRE. I always thought it was hand.

SIMON. It's not.

CLAIRE. Oh. Well whatever it is, it's fucked.

SIMON. Yes. But. Not for much longer.

CLAIRE. Didn't I also say something earlier about a patch-up job? Or is your dead girlfriend getting credit for that too?

SIMON. Once I calmed down I realised maybe it wasn't a total write-off.

I've got all the tapes – masking, gaffer, sello.

I'll use these rods to shore up the frame. Bin bags for the wings.

CLAIRE. Very *Blue Peter.*

SIMON. It's the taking part, isn't it. That's what matters.

CLAIRE. Haven't you missed your slot, though?

SIMON. I explained to one of the organisers – they've moved things around so I can fly tomorrow instead. They've been brilliant, actually. When I explained the circumstances.

CLAIRE. Did you cry at them?

SIMON. No.

CLAIRE. What can I do?

SIMON. What?

CLAIRE. I can hold things, measure things, cut things – whatever you need.

SIMON. Really?

CLAIRE. Why not.

SIMON. I mean, yeah, another pair of hands won't hurt. Thanks.

CLAIRE. Okay then.

Tell me what to do and I'm all yours.

Actually, we probably need some more of this – (*The beer.*) Do you want anything?

SIMON. Won't the people in the shop see you, dob you in to Maeve?

CLAIRE. Fuck 'em. She'll find out soon enough.

What's she seeing?

SIMON. *Titanic.*

CLAIRE. Bit of a sick choice, isn't it.

SIMON. That's what I said.

CLAIRE. Still, it's pretty long. By the time she's back I'll be too pissed to care about the bollocking.

SIMON. Fair enough.

Let me give you some money.

CLAIRE. No.

SIMON. I insist.

He gives her some money from his wallet.

CLAIRE (*re: the beer*). More of the same?

SIMON. Please.

She goes to move away.

Hang on. You've got –

CLAIRE. What?

SIMON. In your hair.

He pulls some of the cake out.

Is it… is it cake?

CLAIRE *pulls some of the crumbs out.*

CLAIRE. Is it gone? Is it in the back? Is it gone?

SIMON. Hold still. Let me…

CLAIRE. Jesus. Get it out, get it all out.

She's clawing at her hair. He's trying to help.

SIMON. It's gone, okay. It's gone. It's gone.

CLAIRE. All of it?

SIMON. Yes.

CLAIRE *stares at him. She'll either crumble or harden. Resolve.*

CLAIRE. I'll be back when I'm back.

Exit CLAIRE outside.

Scene Seven

The guesthouse.

Later.

CLAIRE *and* SIMON *are working on the glider.*

A bottle of wine is on the table along with family-sized packets of crisps, biscuits, snacks.

CLAIRE *gets up to top up her glass.*

SIMON. Are there any of those crisps left?

CLAIRE. Which ones?

SIMON. The hot ones, chilli and something.

> CLAIRE *eats the last handful.*

CLAIRE. Nope, all gone.

> But I might have…

> *She retrieves a supermarket carrier, pulls out more packets of crisps.*

> Ta-dah!

SIMON. How much did you get?

CLAIRE. Sustenance for the workers, isn't it. An army marches on its stomach and all that.

> Here. (*Throws him the crisps.*)

> Do you want another beer?

SIMON. I should stop, really. I don't want a hangover for tomorrow.

CLAIRE. Hardly likely. You've been sipping at that bottle like a teeny-tiny little birdie.

SIMON. I'm a slow drinker.

> *She opens a new bottle of wine and pours herself a glass. She takes him another beer, kicking her trainers off as she goes.*

She surveys their handiwork.

We're getting there.

CLAIRE. Yup. I'm going to tape that on to that, is that right?

SIMON. Show me.

CLAIRE. There to there.

SIMON. No. That to there.

CLAIRE. Copy that.

They work.

SIMON. Maeve's been gone a while.

CLAIRE. She does as she does, does our Mavis.

SIMON. Mavis, yes, sorry.

CLAIRE. It doesn't matter, I only do it to wind her up.

What's your mum called?

SIMON. Shirley.

CLAIRE. That's a great name. Does she have a blonde bubble
    perm and a cleavage you could get lost in?

SIMON. No. She's got vitiligo and too many novelty teapots.

CLAIRE. And prize-winning guinea pigs.

SIMON. Those too.

CLAIRE. Mum'll be on the beach plonked in a deckchair
    spouting film facts to anyone who'll listen. She loves being
    out and about, holding court, I'm just glad she's
    remembering that.

SIMON. When did she have the stroke?

CLAIRE. About three months ago. She went to stay with my
    sister after she got out of hospital. She fussed to get home
    the whole time.

SIMON. Did she lose her speech or...?

CLAIRE. Sadly not.

SIMON. I don't really know anything about strokes.

CLAIRE. I'm quite the expert these days.

So, the right-hand side of the brain controls the left-hand side of the body and vice versa. A right-hand-side stroke, which is what she had, is less likely to cause speech problems, but the paralysis can seem worse. It's like her brain isn't able to recognise her left arm any more. It's disowned it. It's weird.

SIMON. Will it get better?

CLAIRE. I hope so.

SIMON. She seems in good spirits, though. She's quite a character.

CLAIRE. It's knocked her. She was always busy, you know. This place, mainly. Too much lipstick, too much perfume, quick with a joke, nothing's too much trouble.

She didn't give herself time to get properly better, though. Had guests back too soon, had a total meltdown, ended up back in hospital.

I didn't even know she'd reopened. Silly sod.

SIMON. That's why you cancelled everyone.

CLAIRE. Tried to.

SIMON. That's so kind of you – to up sticks, leave your family to look after her.

CLAIRE (*sharp*). Angie was on holiday, I had no choice.

SIMON. Still. Did they not fancy some time by the sea?

CLAIRE. Jamie's job.

SIMON. I'm sure your son –

CLAIRE (*sharp*). Mum was ill. She needed calm, quiet. It was better just me.

CLAIRE *drains her glass – pours herself another one.*

Have you got a name for it? This. You have to give it a name.

What about 'Skyrocket'?

Or, like, the wartime planes that had the pin-ups on the side – 'Daredevil Debbie'. We could paint it across the wings –

SIMON. It's called Tinker Bell.

CLAIRE. Oh. Course.

SIMON. Yeah.

CLAIRE. How long were you and Emmie together?

SIMON. Not long enough. No one ever believes me but we met on a train.

CLAIRE. Why would I not believe you? People go on trains.

SIMON. It was heaving so we were squashed into one of the vestibules.

CLAIRE. Isn't 'vestibule' a great word?

SIMON. We got talking and it turned out we lived pretty near each other.

The trolley wasn't doing the rounds cos the train was so full so she let me share her Ribena. She asked me to write my number on the carton and that was that.

CLAIRE. The article in the paper said it was cancer?

SIMON. Yes. Pancreatic.

CLAIRE. How old was she?

SIMON. Twenty.

CLAIRE. That's so young.

SIMON. Yes.

We went out for a meal, our first date after the train. She started complaining of a stomach ache. Her tummy, her back. She said it was something that came and went, but I insisted we go to A&E. She was in agony.

That was the start of it. Endless referrals, tests, scans.

Eighteen months later she was gone.

CLAIRE. Was there nothing they could do?

SIMON. It was at a really advanced stage when they found it.

She had chemotherapy for a while, but it was just delaying the inevitable.

CLAIRE. But you stuck around, even though…

SIMON. What?

CLAIRE. It's a big ask for a new boyfriend. Not even a boyfriend, a first date with a stranger off a train.

SIMON. You think I should have dropped her off at casualty and run?

CLAIRE. What if it turned out you had nothing in common? What if you didn't like her?

SIMON. I did like her.

CLAIRE. You didn't know her.

SIMON. I did.

CLAIRE. You only knew her when she was ill.

SIMON. So?

CLAIRE. Well. Surely it changes you. A diagnosis like that.

If you didn't know her before –

SIMON. Before didn't matter. We were in the moment, always.

CLAIRE. I suppose I can understand it from her side, getting her claws right in –

SIMON. Excuse me?

CLAIRE. She must have been terrified. Nobody wants to die alone.

SIMON. She was never going to be alone – she had her family, friends.

CLAIRE. Then what were you for?

SIMON. It's a different kind of relationship, isn't it. With a
partner. A different kind of love.

CLAIRE. You loved her?

SIMON. We loved each other.

CLAIRE. From one date?

SIMON. From the vestibule.

They work. CLAIRE *is struggling to cut a pole with scissors.*
SIMON *passes her a stanley knife.*

Here, you'll get on better.

They work.

CLAIRE. Are you pissed off with me?

SIMON. It's nothing I haven't heard before.

CLAIRE. But probably never discussed with my wit and delicacy.

SIMON. No.

CLAIRE. Why this, then? It's a bit of an odd thing to ask you
to do.

SIMON. Is it?

CLAIRE. Asking you to jump off the pier in a novelty flying
competition.

SIMON. This was the last place we came together before she
died. She read about it online. We just got in the car and drove.

It was such a beautiful day. Blue skies, not a cloud.

CLAIRE. Mum said it hoyed it down.

SIMON. No. Not at all. Glorious. The sun made Emmie's hair
shine like gold.

She had a pink top on and dripped ice cream all down the
front. She didn't even realise. She was so wrapped up
watching the flyers – cheering, clapping – she was licking
one half of this massive, double-cone ice cream – a Flake,

monkey's blood, sprinkles, the works – while the other half melted all down her. She just laughed when she saw it.

It was all she could talk about when we got back. Us coming back here this year, me taking part. I honestly think it got us a few more months together. But she just couldn't hang on to see it.

CLAIRE. Can I hear the poem she wrote you?

SIMON. No.

CLAIRE. Come on.

SIMON. No.

CLAIRE. Fine. See if I can guess... 'Roses are red, violets blue, you might drown but that's okay, cos then I'll be with you.'

SIMON....

CLAIRE. Come on. For making it up on the spot, not bad.

SIMON....

CLAIRE. I'm joking.

SIMON. You're being horrible.

CLAIRE. Don't get pissy. I'm just showing an interest. I'm not forcing you to tell me your life story.

SIMON. Why don't you wear a wedding ring?

CLAIRE. What?

SIMON. How did you meet your husband?

Remind me your son's name.

CLAIRE. No.

SIMON. I'm showing an interest, don't get pissy.

CLAIRE. Yeah, alright.

CLAIRE *gets up and moves away. She still has the stanley knife.*

She retrieves SIMON*'s glass which is mostly full.*

SIMON. No more for me. Thank you.

She drains his glass. He watches her.

She finishes her own drink and pours another.

Do you not think you've had enough?

CLAIRE. Not even close.

SIMON. Okay. I think maybe we've done all we can tonight.

CLAIRE. But you have to be ready for tomorrow.

SIMON. I can finish in the morning.

CLAIRE. The Big Jump. The poetry recital.

SIMON. I'll move it back to the van.

Give me a hand, can you please. You take that end… the corner, careful.

CLAIRE. Don't order me about in my own house.

SIMON. I'm not.

Look, I'm sorry if I was sharp with you. You were going a bit far, though.

CLAIRE. If that's your idea of too far.

SIMON. I apologise. We're both tired –

CLAIRE. And it hurt more because you're normally such a sap.

SIMON. Right.

CLAIRE. You're not even going to dispute it?

SIMON. Pass me the stanley knife, can you.

CLAIRE. What?

SIMON. Just, pass it over. I need it for this.

CLAIRE. For what?

SIMON. This. Here.

CLAIRE. There's nothing.

SIMON. Can I have it please.

CLAIRE. You think I'm going to cut you?

SIMON. No.

CLAIRE. You think I'm going to cut myself?

SIMON. No.

She checks that her top is pulled down, that she's covered. She is.

CLAIRE. What have you seen?

SIMON. What? Nothing.

CLAIRE. You fucking snake.

SIMON. What? Calm down.

Here, just –

He steps towards her, wanting the knife. Instinct, she swipes it at him.

Fuck.

CLAIRE. Sorry, no. No.

She realises what she has done, she throws the knife down. They stand for a time, recovering themselves.

SIMON. Okay, look, I'm going to get this thing out of here.

He tries to move the glider. A piece falls off.

Shitting arseing useless bloody thing.

CLAIRE *starts to laugh. He glares at her.*

CLAIRE. Oh come on…

SIMON *laughs in spite of himself.*

SIMON. I'm going down like a stone out there, aren't I?

CLAIRE. I don't want to go home.

The laughter stops. Silence.

SIMON. Why not?

CLAIRE. Why not what?

SIMON. Why don't you want to go home?

CLAIRE. Who told you that?

SIMON....

CLAIRE. At Callum's party today... When I walked in I thought I'd missed the whole thing. No one's in the house, it's quiet, and I think maybe it's not so bad, maybe it's going to be okay. But they're all outside. Jamie's got a bouncy castle in the garden, tables of crisps and pizza, everyone's smiling. He's done it all himself, the castle, the food, the smiling, everything. Cal's bouncing and squealing and Jamie's got an eye on him, proud as punch. He looks right. Like a parent. It fits him. He likes it.

Neither of them notice me at first and I'm glad.

Jamie waited for me before they did the cake. Cos he's gorgeous and considerate like that. He's made it from scratch, this caterpillar. Homemade, not shop. He let Callum say what he wanted and he's made it – the sponge, the filling, iced it, all the detail, he's very proud of it. It's really good, he should be.

Jamie carries it outside, we're all singing, I'm singing, at least I'm moving my mouth, but I can't take my eyes off the candles. The flames are cartoon yellow, massive. I'm staring and the cake is getting brighter, this mass of yellow and flame and it's going to burn him, burn the whole place down, and everyone's singing, and I throw my drink over the cake to put the fire out.

It goes quiet. Snap. Silence.

I rub the sweat off my face and get cake all over myself. I just threw my drink, didn't I? But I look and I'm covered in cream and sponge and jam and radioactive green icing. The cake's destroyed, smashed, where I've slammed my hands through.

I try to wipe it off but it's fused to my skin. I'm clawing at it, tearing off ratty little chunks, and it's ripping off part of me with it.

And they're all looking, the parents, the kids, Jamie. Callum. They're seeing the flesh of me, bleeding and sore. They're seeing that I don't have a bloody clue. That I'm so bored. That all I want to do is stand on the table and yell – 'I don't give a flying fuck about any of this.'

Callum's eyes are wet and massive, and I can't look and I can't keep pretending any more, so I walked out and came back here.

SIMON....

CLAIRE. You think I'm repulsive.

SIMON. I didn't say that. I didn't say anything.

CLAIRE. Forget it. I don't care what you think, I don't know you.

SIMON. Okay.

CLAIRE. Do you think I should go home?

SIMON. You don't care what I think.

CLAIRE. That's a yes then.

SIMON. No.

CLAIRE. He's a gorgeous little boy, he really is. I can see that, as an outsider looking in I'm aware of that, but it doesn't...

I can't breathe when I'm with him, there's a boulder in my stomach.

That's not right, is it. That's not how I should feel.

SIMON. And how's that?

CLAIRE. You know.

SIMON. Tell me.

CLAIRE. Happy. Love.

SIMON. You don't love him?

CLAIRE. I don't not love him.

SIMON. And are you happy now, away from them?

CLAIRE. Right at this moment, not really.

But the thought of being back with them... that's worse.

Saying it out loud, I'm a monster.

SIMON. You're not a monster.

CLAIRE. I am. I know I am.

CLAIRE *pulls up her top, exposing scars on her stomach.*

I started doing it after he was born. Just tiny slices. Then the words started.

SIMON. Jesus Christ.

CLAIRE. I did this one tonight, outside in the car.

She shows him. It says –

Caterpillar.

SIMON. Shit. It looks infected.

Have you got any antiseptic or bandages or...

CLAIRE. It's fine.

Exit SIMON *to the hallway.*

He returns with a basket of cotton wool, antiseptic, plaster dressings. He tends to the cuts.

SIMON. A first-aid kit on every landing.

CLAIRE (*re: the pain*). Oww.

SIMON. Sorry.

CLAIRE. Shit.

SIMON. Nearly done.

Why would you do this?

CLAIRE. I can't walk away from my son unscathed. I haven't let myself.

(*Re: the scars*.) These remind me what I am. That it's not right. I can't be allowed to forget that.

SIMON (*applying the dressing*). Done.

CLAIRE. I need a drink.

She goes to pull her top down.

SIMON. No, don't.

He studies her skin.

Are there more?

CLAIRE. Yes. My thighs, my hips.

SIMON. What does Jamie say?

CLAIRE. He doesn't know.

SIMON. He must have seen.

CLAIRE. No.

SIMON. But –

CLAIRE (*firm*). No.

SIMON. Can I?

He traces his fingers lightly over some of the scars. She lets him.

The landline telephone rings. The answerphone kicks in.

AUTOMATED VOICE. Hello. We are unable to take your call at the moment. Please leave a message after the tone.

BEEEEEEEEP!

JAMIE (*voice*). Maeve, it's Jamie. Sorry to ring so late, but I was wondering if Claire's with you?

CALLUM (*voice, background*). Daddy, daddy.

JAMIE (*voice*). Coming, sweetheart.

CALLUM is crying.

There's nothing to worry about, just if you see her –

CLAIRE gets up and ends the call.

CLAIRE. Shit. Shit. Cal was crying, could you hear?

The phone starts to ring again. It seems louder.

Fuck. I can't. I...

SIMON goes over and pulls the phone socket out of the wall. Silence.

I thought when I told someone they'd rail at me, yell, spit bile and claw my face at how disgusting I am, but you. You're not doing that.

SIMON. No.

CLAIRE. Why not?

SIMON. I don't want to.

CLAIRE. What do you want?

SIMON. Run away with me.

CLAIRE. What?

SIMON. Come on. We can go right now

CLAIRE. Go where?

SIMON. Anywhere. There's a whole wide world out there.

CLAIRE. But. I can't.

SIMON. You can.

Anywhere you like. Just you and me.

CLAIRE. You don't know me.

SIMON. I know something about you no one else does.

And I'll get to know you. This you, from right now onwards. Nothing else before matters.

And you'll know me.

CLAIRE. We can't.

SIMON. Why not?

CLAIRE. Loads of reasons.

SIMON. Name them.

CLAIRE. Your flight.

SIMON. Fuck it.

CLAIRE. What about poor dead Emmie?

SIMON. She's not here, you are.

CLAIRE. She was your golden girl five minutes ago.

SIMON. You're not listening. Five minutes ago doesn't matter.

Isn't that what you want?

We can be free.

CLAIRE. Really?

SIMON. Yes.

CLAIRE. Even though… After everything I've told you?

SIMON. Yes. Yes.

He kisses her scars.

She kisses him, passionate, grateful.

Scene Eight

The guesthouse.

Sunday morning. Very early.

The room and the glider remain as they left them.

The doorbell rings. There is knocking. The bell rings and rings.

Eventually SIMON *appears in his boxers, pulling a T-shirt on.*

He opens the door to MAEVE. *She is dishevelled, exhausted. One side of her face is scratched and sore.*

MAEVE. Can you pay the taxi driver?

SIMON. What?

MAEVE. He's waiting. I don't have my purse, can you pay him?

SIMON *retrieves his wallet and exits outside.*

MAEVE *takes in the room. The empty bottles. The mess.* CLAIRE*'s trainers.*

SIMON *returns.*

Is Claire here?

SIMON. Yes.

MAEVE. Did she go home at all?

SIMON. Yes. But she came back.

MAEVE. Is she okay?

SIMON. Yes.

MAEVE. Why isn't she answering the door?

SIMON. She's spark out. Snoring her head off.

MAEVE. Is she now.

SIMON. What happened to your face?

MAEVE. I think I'm going to be sick.

SIMON. What?

MAEVE. Be sick…

> SIMON *looks for a receptacle. He grabs a fruit bowl, empties it, holds it out for* MAEVE.

> *Her nausea passes.*

SIMON. Alright?

MAEVE. I thought you must have gone off again. I was about to put a rock through the window.

SIMON. I was asleep.

MAEVE. Nice to know you've had the search parties out.

SIMON. You were at the beach watching the film.

MAEVE. Till three in the morning?

SIMON. Is that the time? Shit.

MAEVE. My bloody bag got nicked. A kid on a bike. He had it, there was no need to shove me over – that was just a bonus, topple the old lady.

SIMON. Little bastard.

MAEVE. I couldn't break my fall. They think I blacked out for a sec. Some do-gooder called an ambulance.

SIMON. It looks nasty.

> You should have rung. I'd have come and picked you up.

MAEVE. My phone was in my bag. Purse, keys. I'll have to get the locks changed.

> I tried the house from the hospital payphone but it was always engaged.

SIMON.…

MAEVE. Get me a drink, will you?

SIMON. Of course. Water? Coke? Coke's meant to be good if you're feeling sick.

MAEVE. Coke, yeah. With a vodka in it.

Exit SIMON *to the kitchen.*

(*Calling after him.*) I'm not joking. There's a bottle under the sink.

MAEVE *examines the landline telephone. She notices it is unplugged. She plugs it back in.*

Enter SIMON *with a glass of Coke.*

SIMON. A double. For the shock.

MAEVE *drinks.*

Strong enough?

MAEVE. Yes.

SIMON. Top tip, always ask for your shots to be poured above the counter. Then you see you're getting what you're paying for. I've worked in bars and the scams –

MAEVE. Bartender and delivery boy, my my what a catch.

SIMON. She's a grown woman.

MAEVE. She is, yes. With a husband and a child.

SIMON *scoffs.*

What does that mean?

SIMON. What?

MAEVE. That sound you just made.

SIMON. Did I?

MAEVE. Go on.

SIMON. I'm not sure if I should –

MAEVE. This is my home and you are my guest.

I asked you a question.

SIMON. She's unhappy. She's in a life she doesn't want.

MAEVE. What does that mean?

SIMON. The husband, the child, she doesn't want it.

MAEVE. She told you that?

SIMON. Yes.

MAEVE. Those words?

SIMON. More or less.

MAEVE. Okay. So what does she want? You?

Look at you with your post-shag glow thinking you've unearthed some big secret.

SIMON. You knew?

MAEVE. I know she's struggling.

SIMON. She said she hadn't told anyone else.

MAEVE. She hasn't. But my brain's not totally gone to jelly. She's my daughter, for God's sake. And I'm dealing with it, we don't need you.

SIMON. Oh here we go. Playing the Parent Card.

MAEVE. Pardon me?

SIMON. You're just the same as Emmie's mum and dad, trying to push me out. When I brought her here they went spare, came after us, dragged her back to hospital and machines. What good was any of that doing her? They wouldn't listen either.

I'm helping Claire.

MAEVE. Helping how?

SIMON. Giving her options.

MAEVE. Do you really think you're an alternative to Jamie? That man is a saint.

SIMON. Forcing her to have a kid?

MAEVE. She said that?

SIMON. It's obvious. Superdad with his bouncy castles and his baking. It's all about him, what he wants.

MAEVE. You don't know how they are together, her and him. The three of them. They fit. I wish she could see that.

Suddenly MAEVE *is sick down her front.*

SIMON. Bloody hell.

Exit SIMON *to the kitchen.*

He returns with a cloth.

He wipes her down and tries to take her stained cardigan off. She resists.

Okay, fine, ferment in your own puke.

MAEVE *relents, but still resisting his help.*

I should take you back to the hospital. Being sick after blacking out. Are you sure they gave you the okay?

MAEVE. I discharged myself.

With the cardigan off we see the skin of MAEVE*'s poorly arm for the first time – it is badly bruised.*

SIMON. Jesus.

MAEVE. It looks worse than it is. They said cos my arm was slack it did less damage than if I'd tensed up.

SIMON. All this isn't from a fall tonight.

MAEVE. It is.

SIMON. Some of these are old, Maeve. Some fresh.

MAEVE. You don't know what you're talking about.

SIMON. There's fingermarks. Is this Claire doing this?

MAEVE. No.

SIMON. I'm going to get her.

MAEVE. No. Please.

Please.

SIMON. Then tell me.

MAEVE. She doesn't hurt me. A squeeze, a pinch, a grab –
I don't feel it. I'm not sure she even knows she's doing it.

SIMON. What did the hospital say when they saw?

MAEVE. I said I do it to myself. Trying to wake the arm up, shock it back to life.

SIMON. Did they believe you?

MAEVE. The nurse said it's quite common. She was going to refer me to a psychologist.

SIMON. You're not the one who needs one.

MAEVE. This isn't her. It'll pass.

SIMON. She cuts herself.

MAEVE. What?

SIMON. She scratches words into her skin.

MAEVE. No she doesn't.

Where?

SIMON. All over. You're not the only one covering yourself up.

MAEVE. What kind of words?

SIMON. Bad ones.

MAEVE. Like what? Come on, you've obviously had an eyeful tonight. Read her cover to back.

SIMON. 'Scared', 'Bitch', 'Cold'.

MAEVE. Okay.

SIMON. 'Worst', 'Caterpillar'.

MAEVE. Stop.

Whatever's boiling away inside her, twisting her up –
I thought if I let her lash out at me, get it out of her system.
Kids are hard work. Relentless.

I thought if this helps her get back to him

SIMON. Do you really think a woman who does this should be near her son?

MAEVE. She wouldn't hurt Cal.

SIMON. Are you sure?

MAEVE. Yes.

SIMON *goes to exit to the hallway.*

Where you going?

SIMON. I'm getting her. She should see this.

MAEVE. She's seen it, love.

SIMON. No. She lets you cover it up so she doesn't have to face what she's doing.

MAEVE. She can't know I told you.

SIMON. Fine. I'll say I saw your arm when you got home from the hospital.

MAEVE. And I'll say it's from the fall.

And she'll let me lie and then she'll take you back to bed with her and you'll go.

SIMON....

MAEVE. Maybe it's good, you know. In a way.

SIMON. How?

MAEVE. For her to be tearing herself up like this about it. About Callum. It shows she's a mother, in her heart. It's part of who she is.

And there are moments, I've seen them – moments when they're exactly as they should be. A mother and her son. This is just a wobble. She can get back to that.

SIMON. It's more than a wobble.

MAEVE. She's got a loving family, a lovely home.

She can't feel like this. She can't.

I... I don't know what to do.

SIMON. It's okay.

MAEVE. You know, I didn't think I'd done too badly with
Claire. And Angie. Claire was our first, though, and you're
never sure if you're doing it right. So when she married
Jamie, had Callum, was all settled, I thought 'well done me'.
Cos I did most of it on my own.

SIMON. Did their dad leave?

MAEVE. Yes. They were just teenagers. But it happens. You get
on with it.

SIMON. Can't Jamie 'get on with it'?

MAEVE. It's different.

SIMON. Why?

MAEVE. A mother doesn't leave her child. It's impossible. It's
obscene.

SIMON. It's okay. You've done your best.

I understand.

*He kneels by her, rubbing her bruised arm gently,
supportively.*

He takes her hand, squeezes it, kisses it.

She pulls her hand away.

MAEVE. What are you doing?

SIMON. Helping you.

MAEVE. Get away from me, you creepy little fucker.

SIMON. What?

MAEVE. She slices herself up, but you still gave her one? Why?

SIMON. I was helping her.

MAEVE. With your cock?

SIMON. It wasn't like that.

MAEVE. Of course not. You're two lost souls who've found
each other, can heal each other. Am I right?

SIMON. We had a connection.

MAEVE. 'Had'? Past tense? But not now?

SIMON. I don't… I didn't know she…

MAEVE. I don't think you like that she's still got some teeth, that she's not the feeble victim you hoped.

I see you, boy.

SIMON *moves away. Caught?*

MAEVE *regroups*.

Everyone cuts themselves these days, don't they. If you haven't got at least one silvery scar on your arm then you're clearly not doing it properly.

SIMON. Not doing what?

MAEVE. Life.

Living.

She'll be fine.

SIMON. What if she's not?

MAEVE. She'll have to be.

This is classic Claire, if she's not good at something straight away she ditches it. She was the same with hockey, and we'd bought her all the kit.

SIMON. I really don't think –

MAEVE. Look, I'm not well enough to have guests. Everyone's telling me I'm doing too much, they're right.

Pack up your things, please. I want you, and that, out of my house.

SIMON. It's 3 a.m.

MAEVE. Go back to bed, your own bed, don't disturb Claire. But I want you gone first thing, I don't want either of us to lay eyes on you again.

He goes to exit to the hallway. Pauses.

SIMON. What if she can't love Callum?

MAEVE. Don't you say his name.

SIMON. What if she doesn't want to?

Exit SIMON.

MAEVE *is left alone. She is suddenly dizzy, disorientated. She tries to call out but can only manage a slurred noise. She sits heavily down on to the settee.*

Scene Nine

Outside.

Later Sunday morning.

CLAIRE *sits on the bench. She has the local paper. She tears out a page and starts trying to make a paper plane.*

After a time, enter SIMON. *He is dressed as Peter Pan. It's a shop-bought fancy-dress costume, good quality. But he still looks a tit.*

He sees her. She sees him.

There's no getting out of it.

CLAIRE. You're in the paper again.

SIMON. Am I?

CLAIRE. A nice photo of Emmie. She's not what I thought.

SIMON. What did you think?

CLAIRE. I'm not sure.

SIMON. Beauty like hers, it's hard to do justice to.

CLAIRE. I thought you'd done a runner when I woke up. Glider gone. Van gone.

SIMON. I drove it down to the pier first thing. Wanted to get a spot.

CLAIRE. Right.

SIMON. I should get down there, I need to sign in.

CLAIRE. You're still jumping then?

SIMON. Yes.

CLAIRE. Otherwise that's quite a bold look for church, I suppose.

Silence.

Uncomfortable.

SIMON *retrieves a folded sheet of paper. He's careful/reverent with it.*

Is that the fabled poem?

SIMON. Yes.

CLAIRE. You need to paper-plane it.

You can show me. I'm making a right pig's ear of this.

He sits next to her. He folds the poem into a paper plane.

She copies what he does with a page of the newspaper.

SIMON. That's too big. Quarter it down. Fold it so there's a crease in the middle.

Fold down the top two corners.

These corners, fold them again. That's right.

Fold it in half. Fold, to make a wing.

Done. Ready for take-off.

She throws her plane. It's crap.

SIMON *goes to retrieve it, leaving his plane poem on the bench.* CLAIRE *retrieves it, unfolds it.*

Newspaper's too thin. You need something more substantial.

CLAIRE (*reading*). 'Emmie. Did you love me?
Did you even like me?
What am I meant to do now?
I'm sorry.'

It doesn't even rhyme.

SIMON. I did get your cancellation email. I was quite relieved actually, but I found I couldn't stop myself. I just kept ploughing forward with all the plans and as this weekend got closer I knew I had to still come.

CLAIRE. You don't know if she even liked you? Everything you've said –

SIMON. When we were here last year, she went on and on that the water stank. It doesn't stink, does it.

CLAIRE. No.

SIMON. She sat folded up on this bench the whole time, a face on her. How tired she was, cold, it was wet, noisy, she didn't feel well. When I came back with ice creams for us, the way she looked at me. Lactose intolerant. Ninety-nines gave her the shits.

I ate hers and mine.

When I went for a piss she rang her parents to come and get her. I thought her stepdad was going to chin me. The things he said – I was a nuisance, a pest, I had to leave her alone. I was the good guy, you know, but she… she just let him.

After they left I stayed and watched the flyers. I thought it was all a bit pointless, to be honest.

I didn't see her again. I tried, but there was never a chance, there was always someone with her.

I read it on Facebook that she'd died. Her sister posted it. I didn't even see it straight away, like hours later.

There was no last request. Emmie never wanted anything from me. I didn't matter enough for that.

I never meant to… all of this… not really. But it's spiralled and I'm trapped.

CLAIRE. Last night you were willing to walk away, easy as anything.

SIMON. The thought of jumping off that pier, though.

Apparently it only takes eighty-seven seconds underwater before you start to drown.

I wonder if it feels like ages or like nothing. What have I got in my life to think about in that time, before I die? Her. There's only her.

CLAIRE. Me?

SIMON. What?

CLAIRE. Last night –

SIMON. I was drunk.

CLAIRE. No you weren't.

SIMON. You were.

CLAIRE. We'll put all this behind us. A new start for us both, remember.

It doesn't have to last. I'm not asking for any big commitment, marriage or… I mean, come on.

It gets us away, though, doesn't it. It's a reason. It's not 'I left my kid,' it's 'I met someone else.'

SIMON.…

CLAIRE. You said things. You, Simon. I never asked you to.

Simon.

SIMON. I know I did.

I thought I could, I want to but…

You're not what I thought.

CLAIRE. What do you mean?

She reaches for him, he shrugs her off.

SIMON. My Emmie was never clingy or needy.

She didn't lash out.

My Emmie was strong and brave. Or delicate and scared.

She didn't have scars, she was flawless. Peaches and cream, or tanned and glowing, or pale and gaunt, or whatever I say she was.

CLAIRE. But that's not real.

SIMON. Good.

CLAIRE. I thought you were going to save me.

SIMON. So did I. But you have to be worth saving.

Emmie was worth it. And even if she wasn't, I can say she was and there's no one to contradict me.

I'm not ready to let that go.

CLAIRE. That poor girl. You sucking the life out of her when she had so little left anyway. I bet she rued the day she got on that train.

SIMON. Go home, Claire. Be a mother. Be a human.

SIMON *exits.*

CLAIRE *remains.*

She retrieves her packet of cigarettes and pats herself down for a lighter.

After a time, MAEVE *enters. She wears sunglasses to try and cover the damage to her face. Is she more delicate than she was? Last night was a setback.*

MAEVE *has a plastic carrier bag, and a bunch of helium party balloons on string. She approaches* CLAIRE.

MAEVE. Can I have one of those? (*A cigarette.*)

CLAIRE. You don't smoke.

MAEVE. I wanna look cool.

CLAIRE. You wish.

> CLAIRE *passes her one*.

> Do you have a lighter?

MAEVE. No. I don't smoke.

> CLAIRE *takes the cigarette back and shoves it in the packet*.

> When did you get back?

CLAIRE. Just now.

MAEVE. Everything okay?

CLAIRE. Fine.

MAEVE. I see our guest has gone.

CLAIRE. Has he?

MAEVE. I woke up and he'd cleared out. Keys on the table.

CLAIRE. Oh well.

MAEVE. We're okay aren't we, love?

CLAIRE. What do you mean?

MAEVE. You and me, how we are. I know we don't hug and
kiss and braid each other's hair, but you know if there's
anything you ever want to talk about...

> CLAIRE *doesn't answer*.

> Am I a good mother?

CLAIRE. Depends who else is in the category.

MAEVE. Am I?

CLAIRE. Yes.

MAEVE. I do my best, you know that?

CLAIRE. Course.

MAEVE. Cos that's all you can ask, isn't it. To do your best.
To try.

Pause. CLAIRE *is frozen. An understanding.*

CLAIRE. Yes.

MAEVE. Jamie rang the house before. I told him I'd tried to run before I could walk – typical – that I was still a bit fragile. I said I'd asked you to come back.

CLAIRE. Okay.

Thanks.

MAEVE. He's coming over.

CLAIRE. Here?

MAEVE. Yes. They've set off. They might see the tail-end of the competition if they make good time.

You can all stay with me, blow the cobwebs off, then head back together.

It's the best thing.

CLAIRE (*looking at* MAEVE *for the first time*). Maeve, I –

CLAIRE *sees the balloons.*

What are they?

MAEVE. I thought we could have a little birthday party for Callum.

CLAIRE. He's had his party.

MAEVE. Another one won't hurt. Everyone likes two parties, stretch it out.

I've got hats, party poppers. We can get fish and chips. Sit out in the garden if this weather holds. Just us. That'll be nice.

CLAIRE. What's wrong with your face?

MAEVE. It's fine.

CLAIRE. What happened?

MAEVE. I fell over. Last night, on the way back from the film, I tripped.

CLAIRE. Things to look out for, loss of balance –

MAEVE. I tripped.

CLAIRE. Clumsiness then, spatial awareness. You know what the hospital said. Relapses, maybe even just small, they're not uncommon.

MAEVE. No.

A loose paving stone, that's all.

CLAIRE. Promise?

MAEVE. Yes.

CLAIRE *moves away, looks out to the pier.*

CLAIRE. They're starting to congregate.

There's a right bell-end dressed as Peter Pan.

MAEVE. Let's see.

Is that…?

CLAIRE. He's scared he's going to drown, you know. Simon.

MAEVE. One can but hope.

CLAIRE. Forget the landing, though. Imagine the flight. Being stretched out in that great big empty space.

I can't think of anything better.

MAEVE. Jamie will have set off by now.

CLAIRE. You've already said that.

MAEVE. Yes.

CLAIRE. Never think I don't care.

MAEVE. What?

CLAIRE. I can… I mean, I have the ability to care.

MAEVE. I know you do.

CLAIRE. I came here to look after you. *That's* why I came. Cos you're my mum.

MAEVE. I know that.

I know.

MAEVE *hugs* CLAIRE *tight*. CLAIRE *returns the embrace*.

In the distance, lively music starts up.

Scene Ten

Outside. The edge of the pier.

Later.

CLAIRE *stands holding the bunch of helium birthday balloons.*

CLAIRE. Walking along before you arrived, I noticed the word 'Tinker Bell' glint in the sun, the paint still a bit wet, probably pilfered off another entrant moved by the ever-elaborate sob story.

He threw his plane, his pathetic unanswered questions. It nosedived straight into the water. He followed close behind with an undignified belly-flop. A collective 'ouch' from the crowd.

What a tribute.

These balloons wouldn't pass muster of course, not next to the *hang*-gliders and pedal-powered planes and superhero capes. But then, I'm too late for an official entry. Everyone's packed up and gone, just all their rubbish left behind to know they were ever here.

I told Daddy and Nana that I was nipping out for a minute, get some air, I had a headache. They smiled at me, smiles that didn't make it to their eyes, and nodded. I ruffled your hair as I went past you. You laughed and put your hand up to mine. But you didn't watch me go. None of you did.

I think – does this make sense? – I think my body is preparing itself. My blood is getting thinner, my bones are hollowing out. I feel lighter. The pull is getting stronger, lifting me up then putting me down. The breeze is getting up but it won't take me, it needs me to make the leap.

Will I get high enough to look back over the roofs into the garden and see you? I'd like that. You might not believe me, but I really would. One last time.

You'll be smiling. Of course you will, with a daddy who loves you, who makes sure you see clouds in your sleep and know it's all yours for the taking, all the caterpillar cakes you can eat. And I'll smile too. And that's okay.

My toes scrape along the wood, nearer still to the edge. I'm teetering. Sink or swim. Flight or fall. I look out to the blue. I'm ready.

End.

A Nick Hern Book

Caterpillar first published in Great Britain as a paperback original in 2018 by Nick Hern Books Limited, The Glasshouse, 49a Goldhawk Road, London W12 8QP, in association with Small Truth Theatre, Theatre503 and Michelle Barnette Productions

Caterpillar copyright © 2018 Alison Carr

Alison Carr has asserted her right to be identified as the author of this work

Front cover image: Yasmeen Arden

Designed and typeset by Nick Hern Books, London
Printed in the UK by Mimeo Ltd, Huntingdon, Cambridgeshire PE29 6XX

A CIP catalogue record for this book is available from the British Library

ISBN 978 1 84842 794 5

www.nickhernbooks.co.uk

facebook.com/nickhernbooks

twitter.com/nickhernbooks